To Meriel and Penny
For all the encouragement

1

The computer screen flickered with yellow letters and a hidden hand scrupulously underlined all the words I had been misspelling for decades. It was my last story. Outside in the street, straggling processions of tourists were following the waving umbrellas of their guides. Every corner of the old city was now being invaded by these groups, seven million people every year. The pavements were bustling, the car parks were full and there were queues outside the tea-rooms; overheard conversations could be in Spanish or Japanese. I remembered it had not always been like this. Once upon a time it was an undiscovered place full of historic reminders of the past, secret places that residents were only too happy to share with visitors. A solitary stranger hesitating on a street corner was never lost for long — there was always someone eager to help: 'The Minster . . . ? Straight ahead and turn right. You can't miss it.'

And one hoped he or she would not be disappointed coming upon that venerable pile girdled about by scaffolding and looking like some wounded warrior on crutches. The once pristine white limestone of the West Front was begrimed by the belching fumes of the steam locomotives racing north. And once inside the cathedral, the visitor's sense of awe would quickly be overcome by the air of all pervading gloom: the battle flags of old Yorkshire regiments hanging in tatters from the roof, moth eaten and decayed, sad, dingy and forgotten; the cathedral then was like the city — tired and weary after a long war. For me the recovery from that war-time gloom began with that American marching band. The war had just ended and the Americans joined the victory parade through the city. To us teenagers all things American were new and exciting, they had a brash energy and confidence about them that made you think that things would now be different.

I remembered there had been whispers — the American band did not play 'proper' marching tunes like our regimental bands, they played 'jazz'. That sort of music could not be allowed in the sacred precincts of the cathedral. So after the service the impressively tall American bandsmen lined up outside the cathedral with their shiny instruments and marched silently away with only the soft tap-tap of a solitary drum to mark their step. The crowds watched in funereal silence but when the band reached the narrow streets in the city centre it happened. The big bass drummer twirled his sticks. He gave his drum two tremendous double thumps and the band crashed into life:

'Ta rara ra ra!'

The strains of the St Louis Blues rattled the windows and bounced off the walls. 'Wake up you lot,' the band seemed to be shouting: 'The Yanks are here! Wake up! Wake up!'

It was a blast of fresh air from a different, vibrant, self confident world and it was so startling and so exciting that as a young boy I wanted to shout: 'Yes! Yes! Yes!'

In the centre of the band was a black soldier with a huge white Sousa-phone coiled around his body, its horn waving proudly high above his head. He was not marching, he was swaggering along and swinging the horn from side to side in time to the music as the band roared its way through the city streets. It was exhilarating. It shook the cobwebs off the old streets, but after they had marched away the dust soon settled back down again. The old city needed more than one American marching band to shake itself awake — but at least it was a start. I looked back on so many stories written since then as a city slowly came back to life after the war years.

2

If I had not been colour blind, of course none of it would have happened — being a journalist that is. Lights flashed in a darkened room.

'What colour's that,' said a voice in the shadows.

'A sort of pink.'

'And this one?'

'I think that's yellow.'

All the lights came on.

'Sorry lad, you're colour blind. We can't employ you.'

So I did not become a mechanical engineer on the railways and instead I became a copy boy on the local newspaper because as my mother said: 'John is good at composition.' Not that I did much writing. I ran with copy from the upstairs subs room to the linotype machines in the basement, once crashing into the editor on the stairs in my enthusiasm; the collision did neither of us any harm. The great man even let it be known that he admired my keenness. That keenness had to survive two years of National Service before I was back again but this time employed in the reporters' room and able to take the stairs at a more leisurely pace. Newly demobbed I had became a floating male at the innumerable evening dress dances that were the vogue after the austerity of war. It was the done thing however at the more formal occasions to go in pairs. Peter the office's self-proclaimed expert on social matters asked me to make up numbers and arranged a blind date.

'She's called Meriel. You'll like her.'

I did. She was tall, slim, blonde and very pretty but also very expensively dressed. Her father, I learned, was a well-to-do farmer and more to the point he would be picking her up and taking her home immediately after the dance. She was a marvellous dancer and we had a great time and during the last waltz we danced a little bit closer. At the end of the evening I escorted her from the ballroom and she retrieved her luxurious beaver lamb coat from the cloakroom. Outside a gleaming Rover car was waiting with a stout, grey-haired gentleman behind the wheel. He gave me the curtest of nods, the car door was opened and my dance partner was driven off into the night like Cinderella leaving the ball in her coach.

Overawed by the whole evening it took some goading by Peter to convince me that there was any point in telephoning.

'Who's calling?' said the voice at the end of the phone which was embarrassing when I had to explain. The silence that followed was even more embarrassing.

'You took your time,' said Meriel. 'I must have made a real impression on you.'

But of course she had and a year later we were married; London was our honeymoon destination but unfortunately it was closed. Queen Mary, our new young Queen's grandmother had died four days before our wedding so most of the London shops were shut or draped in black. The nation was in mourning which was not an auspicious start for a honeymoon.

We spent the first two days looking at the sights while 120,000 people filed past the old queen's coffin as it lay in state in Westminster Abbey. We decided not to join them. In such an atmosphere it was difficult to be cheerful even on honeymoon. London was shabby, and dirty with the scars of the bombing still visible. The tube stations were bleak, uneasy places with the gush of air from the approaching trains blowing rubbish along the platforms. And then there were the bells mournfully tolling for Queen Mary's funeral.

We went to a variety show to cheer ourselves up. The star turn was a girl twirling tassels on the ends of her bosom. For the grand finale she rotated the tassels in opposite directions. Was this the best entertainment the capital could offer?

With the rain falling steadily we abandoned our honeymoon making our respective parents fear the worst. Spirits were not lifted when we returned to our new home, a small semi-detached that we had lovingly decorated and painted in the months before the wedding. There was however no central heating and it was freezing. The front door faced the prevailing wind and strong gusts blew the flap of the letter-box horizontal directing a freezing shaft of icy air down the hall. The warped, iron-framed windows were no better admitting chilling draughts particularly in the bedroom. But this was our home and I was determined to make it cosy so I installed the very latest in double glazing — large sheets of brittle plastic cut to size and held in place with sticky tape. It was very successful until one night there was a rattle and a huge bang that awakened nightmare memories of a visit from the Luftwaffe. Something fell across the bed. Had we been bombed? No, it was the double glazing that had taken flight, blasted from its moorings by the build-up of window draughts.

So we moved from the 'master bedroom' to

the smaller back bedroom where the wind did not howl so much and there was a hot water tank in an airing cupboard giving out blessed warmth. We got dressed and undressed huddled against the tank.

But despite it all we were the young swingers, a new couple about town. We had a washing machine and a television set. Mother came to stare at the clothes going round and round in the washing machine and had difficulty in concealing her envy even though she was not convinced about 'the contraption's' efficiency.

'Can't possibly get things as clean as the old possie-tub,' she said.

After the austerity of the war years things were changing but as a new housewife Meriel still had to struggle with rationing — only half a pound of sugar a week and I had a sweet tooth! Fortunately for me, tea and sweet rationing soon ended but bacon and meat rationing went on for another year.

But among all the changes in the post-war years it was the television set that caused the greatest stir. It was a wedding present from a rich relative, my Uncle Tom. The set was huge and sat brooding in the corner of the lounge like an alien monster. Despite its bulk it only had a tiny, ten inch, flickering, black and white screen; it was however the only television in our street. When the day of the young Queen's Coronation arrived we were surprised to discover what a wide circle of friends and relatives we had. They all came and squashed themselves into the lounge. The momentous events in Westminster Abbey were watched in reverential silence in semi-darkness with the curtains tightly drawn to enhance the television image; Meriel and I tip-toed in and out with cups of tea. We were the lucky ones — we had a television!

3

York was my work place, a proud city with a history going back to the Romans but in many ways it was an overgrown village; the same faces appeared in many roles — as councillors, business people, magistrates or chairman of ancient guilds all obsessively proud of the city's traditions and its ancient ways of doing things. As a young reporter this both fascinated and irritated me. The Lord Mayor for instance was a Right Honourable and his sword bearer had the right to keep his cap on in front of the Queen. In fact the city's sword bearers had been defiantly keeping their caps on in front of royalty ever since Richard III was on the throne. It was, I discovered, no ordinary cap but a Cap of Maintenance trimmed with ermine and kept only for special occasions. All these things the young reporter had to know and respect including the full names and titles of all the local earls, lords and barons. It was after all the age of deference.

The Yorkshire Post, the prestigious county paper once described (as its readers were often reminded) as being one of the world's great newspapers, wanted a young reporter for their district office in the city. It was a wrench leaving the local newspaper for there was a buzz about the place, the smells of ink and hot metal type were exciting. Every afternoon the great printing presses would slowly start turning and the whole building trembled as they reached full power and the papers came tumbling out. That sound was the fulfilment of a day's work: something new being created fresh and different every day. In my new job in a district office I was isolated from all that and I missed it — the heart of my 'great newspaper' beat just as fast but some twenty miles away in Leeds.

There were two newly returned war veterans in my new office, both RAF. Walter, the Chief Reporter, had flown in Mosquito aircraft on intruder raids deep into Europe and there was George the photographer who had been a bomber pilot. I sensed tension between them and soon discovered why: Walter had been a navigator while George had been a pilot. That should have established the pecking order but it did not because George had spent most of his war service training pilots in Canada while Walter, the navigator, had actually flown combat missions. As the office junior I listened enviously to their reminiscences. But quietly I felt very proud too. I was now a journalist on an important newspaper — an official observer, reporter and commentator. It was my job to know everything that was happening in this city, so our readership could be fully informed and this meant attending courts and council meetings, inquests and social events and above all getting to know that small group of people who effectively ran the city.

As I flitted between meetings and social occasions the town characters began to emerge. I was impressed by the Lord Mayor's butler, more of a personage than many of the Lord Mayors. Lean faced and authoritative, Bill would hold court in his pantry at the back of the Mansion House every Monday morning telling us about the Lord Mayor's engagements for the week and all the local gossip. And then there were the council leaders, Labour and Conservative, locked in a see-sawing struggle for power at every election. The social classes were here clearly defined — an astute railwayman led Labour and a sharp local businessman headed the Conservatives. Both were eager to be friendly to the reporters but our office rules were clear: all reporting particularly of political activities had to be 'balanced and fair.' The golden rule was: Facts are sacred,

Comment is free: in other words no bias in the news columns — something which became quaintly even laughingly old fashioned in the decades that followed. Slowly I and the fellow reporter on the other papers became part of the local scene ourselves.

Sitting beside me in the press box on my first day in the magistrates' court was a very old man at least he looked old to me compared with the other young reporters crammed onto the Press seats. He was introduced to me as Noel Blenkin and I watched in admiration as his pencil flew across his notebook writing perfect short-hand. The magistrates, one of them a familiar face in the regional trade union movement, adjourned to consider their verdict. It was then that Noel came to life: 'If they have any sense they will make an example of this character,' he said nodding towards the man in the dock. 'Jail is what he wants. Too much of this sort of thing going on. Magistrates should make an example of him.'

We were overawed by his air of authority. The magistrates returned and the trade union leader spoke to the prisoner in the dock: 'You will be fined £10.'

'Bloody ridiculous,' exploded Noel, slamming down his pencil. The whole court was startled. The press box froze. To my astonishment it was the trade union leader who was the most alarmed. Up on the bench he towered above us but now he was leaning forward anxiously.

'You don't understand, Mr Blenkin,' he said. 'We are very limited in the punishments that we can impose for this sort of offence.'

Noel folded his arms and stared fixedly at the ceiling. The clerk of the court coughed and sorted his papers. In the press box Mr Blenkin slowly picked up his pencil and made an entry in his notebook accompanied by a stage whisper heard by everyone: 'Fined £10.'

'Next case,' said the clerk tactfully.

I learned why everyone knew and respected Mr Blenkin. He had won the Military Cross for bravery in the First World War and had been a colonel in the second. As well as being the town's freelance journalist he was very much a gentleman. As a naive cub reporter I thought he was far too old for such a precarious hand-to-mouth existence as a freelance until I realised the 'system.' Three groups of reporters worked in the city for different papers and all were on the friendliest of terms for mutual preservation purposes; for Noel there was therefore a 'special arrangement.' A 'black' or carbon copy of any big story that might be of interest to the national newspapers was quietly pushed through his letter box. In this way the elderly freelance and local hero could be helped. Everyone had a soft spot for Noel even the police, but there was little the police could do when he left his car parked outside our office without applying the hand brake. It ran backwards down the street and into a shop window. Fortunately no-one was hurt.

The town's assistant chief constable, another friendly figure we all knew well in our overgrown village, prosecuted sympathetically, blaming a faulty hand-brake on the vintage car. The magistrates asked about previous convictions: 'Is there anything known against Mr Blenkin?' To which the assistant chief constable replied, with a wink towards the press box: 'There is nothing known against Mr Blenkin *in this city*, your worships.'

A nominal fine was imposed. It was not mentioned that Mr Blenkin had forgetfully failed to apply his hand-brake on his car only a few weeks before in Scarborough and had been prosecuted and fined. But as the assistant chief constable said that was: 'not in this city, your worships.'

From the office style sheet I had to learn the correct batting order of all the aristocracy, how they should be styled and how they should be addressed. This was important because the aristocracy was a powerful presence all around us on the bench in the courts and chairing meetings; they were still powerful and therefore important.

For the funeral of a local lord every doorway of the cathedral had to be manned by reporters taking names that filled two pages of the paper next day and there were complaints if someone was missed. A supplementary list appeared later with an apology for their late inclusion. At a conference in the city I was behind one smartly dressed gentleman queuing up for his name tag.

'Name please,' asked the flustered girl giving out the tags.

'Feversham,' came the reply.

The girl searched the table in vain and finally asked.

'Could I have your first name?'

'Lord,' was the answer.

4

I was enjoying my role as one of the city reporters for the prestigious county newspaper and I had now acquired a car. My new position as a journalist impressed my bank manager and at a formal 'begging' interview I was loaned £400 with stern warnings about repayments. These came from my £10 a week salary from which was also allocated one pound a week to buy four gallons of petrol. The car was a Ford Popular, the cheapest on the market and cost £399 without hub caps which were classed as a luxury extra. Coming on top of the washing machine and the television my mother and father were appalled. For them it seemed that the whole order and expectations of life were changing. What were we doing with a car at our age? A car was only acquired after long, frugal saving and was bought, if one was lucky, late in life to enjoy trips out when one retired. And then we boldly bought a caravan even though our car only had three forward gears and was seriously underpowered for the task.

With our personal transport and accommodation secured it was inevitable that we ended up on a beach site not far from the harbour in Pwllheli in North Wales. I was drawn there as if by a magnet pulled back into another world that I was emotionally reluctant to enter again. The cormorants were still perched on the mooring poles in the harbour drying their outstretched wings; in fact, everything was as I remembered it as a war-time evacuee including the smell of tar from the rusting gasometer by the railway station.

The Welsh have a word for it *hiraeth* — a nostalgic longing for home. Mother was born in Pwllheli which was how I became an evacuee there during the war. I found the blacked out little town melancholy and depressing, full of sad old people. Even at the risk of being bombed back in Newcastle I wanted to escape. But to my surprise and annoyance when I did get away I discovered that *hiraeth* was infectious. I could not get the damn place out of my mind, in particular the smell of fresh bread always brought it back, memories of the little baker's shop in the High Street and the grey, wisp-like presence of my Auntie Katie behind the wooden counter. I remembered the wartime family gatherings in the tiny gas-lit room behind the shop, everyone chattering in Welsh and the late grand arrival for his supper of Uncle Bob, the baker. Single-handedly he cooked the bread for most of the Lleyn peninsula. He saved my sanity by making me his baker's boy and I had life-abiding memories of him with his long paddle poles sliding the bread tins out of the fiery heat of the ovens and the crackling-fresh loaves tumbling out onto the tables.

Going back on holiday I took Meriel into the bakery where his two nephews were now in residence not the burly, bushy eye-browed character that I remembered. The bakers chatted and winked at Meriel.

'Apprentice come back for a job has he?' they said laughing and nodding towards me. And as they talked they worked, each hand rolling and pummelling dough just as their uncle had done. Although I was on holiday I always felt melancholy because the place was so full of memories and they all seemed to be sad ones. When we turned the car and caravan for home we always drove past the bread shop and there was Auntie Katie standing outside in her black Victorian dress forlornly waving goodbye and looking like a pale ghost from another time. It had to be the Welsh blood in me for every time at that moment an infuriating sadness always crashed over me; it was only when we crossed the border into England that the other half of my family came to the rescue and morbid thoughts were banished. Images of my other ancestors, fierce, claymore-wielding Scots stirred my blood. Come on, get a grip! What had I to be miserable about? But as the mountains faded from the horizon a small voice always whispered in my ear: 'You can't escape that easily. You'll be back.'

5

Back home too many things seemed to be happening. The Editor was on the phone which was a shock because his instructions usually came through minions. I was instructed to interview one of the local lords. 'When?' I asked.

'Now,' he said. 'He's just got back from South Africa and says he's got something important to say about the political situation over there — apartheid and all that.'

I thought South Africa was a little outside my field of expertise but I did not argue.

'He's expecting you in about an hour.'

'When do you want the story?'

'Tonight of course. I'll warn the news desk it's coming.'

That was the way things were done at that time: the county aristocracy crooked a finger and people obeyed; I headed for the broad acres mentally working out how much mileage I would make. I drove through the lodge gates and parked my new Ford Popular (the one without luxury hub caps) on the pebble drive in front of a grand country house. I knocked on the great front door and confidently explained to the butler that I was from the Yorkshire Post and had an appointment to see his lordship. If his lordship was astonished or disappointed at having such a youth in such a car responding to his summonses he graciously did not show it. I sat bolt upright in an armchair in his cosy study while he recounted his trip to Africa. Dutifully I made a note of every word. The story was about a secret radio station broadcasting 'sedition' into South Africa from neighbouring countries and stirring up trouble for the white government which was then trying to hold the line against the abolition of apartheid. My unspoken critical reaction was: 'So what?'

'And I have it on very good authority,' said his lordship, 'that this radio station is being funded from communist sources — Russia!'

In those dark days of the Cold War this was dire news indeed, was the red menace that had half of Europe in its grasp, spreading its tentacles into Africa? I felt duty bound to ask a searching question.

'But how is this known the Russians are involved?'

'I have it on very good authority.'

His lordship had this on very good authority; what more could one say? I tried to get more details about this revelation but his

Lordship's sources were secret — were not his Lordship's assurances enough?

'You will stay for supper.'

It was more of a command than an invitation and also a clear indication that the interview was over. I glanced nervously at the ornate clock on the mantelpiece. Time was ticking away but we adjourned to a vast dining room and were joined by her ladyship. The butler hovered discreetly. His lordship sat at one end of the oval shaped mahogany table her ladyship at the other. I was motioned to a solitary chair set at the centre. A nod from her ladyship and the butler abandoned his moorings alongside an ornate sideboard and circumnavigated the table with a silver dish holding bread buns. We each chose one. The butler returned to the sideboard and voyaged out again with a platter of sliced cold roast beef. Her ladyship selected one slice and so did I. The silence was oppressive. We waited while there was yet another perambulation of the dining room this time with small sticks of celery in a silver jug. Her ladyship broke bread and the feast began.

'Have you been with the Yorkshire Post long?' said his lordship affably. I had never made small talk with a lord before. Journalistic practice however had already taught me something about small talk: let them do the talking. Every now and then a polite open-ended question could be asked but then shut up and listen.

I declined coffee pleading rapidly approaching deadlines and his lordship was astonished to hear that publication was planned for the next day. We shook hands and the butler showed me out. I followed him silently through the great hall, the front door was unlocked and opened and the butler murmured: 'Good evening sir,' as he closed it behind me; my Ford Popular waited for me in the drive.

Darkness was approaching and I found a telephone box outside a post office in a tiny ill-lit village and put in a reverse charge call. The office switchboard operator was suspicious: 'Where did you say you were calling from?'

The news desk was sniffy too.

'We've been waiting for this. Where have you been?'

'His lordship insisted that I stayed to dine.'

'Oh there's posh! Just get the damn copy through.'

Next day it made a very small paragraph on the front page.

6

A trip in George's car always had a whiff of adventure about it. He clearly missed the excitement and the throbbing roar of the four-engine Halifax bomber he flew during the war. His ancient car was a poor substitute for an aeroplane but he drove it as if take-off could be achieved with just a little more throttle. When a youthful Archbishop of York decided to go up in a hot air balloon from his palace gardens at Bishopthorpe, George the photographer was not satisfied with a picture of the Archbishop waving cheerfully as he soared up into the sky.

'Let's get the landing,' he said to me. 'He might get tipped out into a ditch. Great picture!'

So off we went chasing a hot air balloon. Surprisingly for a man of his sharp temperament George had a Yorkshire terrier which he adored and judging by the smell the car was the dog's second home. It sat on the shelf behind the back seat ferociously wagging its tail in welcome when passengers approached. Once settled in their seat the passenger was greeted even more affectionately. Paws were laid on their shoulders and a wet, slobbering tongue enthusiastically cleaned their ears.

'Sit!' George would shout and the dog would retreat cringing to the back window shelf before creeping forward again and giving the passenger's neck another furtive lick. I put up with these displays of affection to save the poor thing from being shouted at. The balloon drifted away and George's hunting instincts were aroused. Fortunately the flying Archbishop drifted clear of the town so we could follow on country roads but then we found the wind was not blowing in the same direction as the roads. We screeched around corners and down side roads trying to keep up. On the back seat shelf the Yorkshire terrier dug in his claws but could not prevent itself from sliding frantically from side to side. Alarmingly too George spent more time peering into the sky than watching the road.

'Look out!' I shouted as a T junction appeared. The brakes were slammed on and something warm, furry and yelping wrapped itself around my neck; it flopped onto my shoulder and collapsed into my lap. The dog however recovered quicker than I did. Bracing its hind legs painfully into my groin its front paws went up onto the dashboard so it could get a better view.

'Yap, yap, yap,' it barked. The damn thing

was enjoying the chase.

'Sit!' roared George, hurling the car to the left still in pursuit of the balloon which was now rapidly losing height. The dog scrabbled painfully across my lap and disappeared through the gap between the two front seats and sulked in the well of the car. Somehow we found a country lane going in the same direction as the balloon.

'It's down,' shouted George and he was out of the car in a flash and running across a field with his cumbersome quarter plate press camera. I followed and saw the canopy of the balloon collapsing half a field away. The landing had been sedate and the basket was standing erect.

'Sod it!' swore George sorely disappointed. The flying Archbishop had not been tipped out in a sprawling clerical heap to make a sensational front page picture for the Yorkshire Post. Instead the Archbishop was looking very calm and pleased with himself leaning over the lip of his wicker basket 'pulpit' as the media rushed towards him.

His Grace gave a lyrical account of the silence and beauty of the Yorkshire country-side as experienced from a hot air balloon: 'the only sound was the mooing of cows. So peaceful.'

The Archbishop's car appeared having

followed at a much more leisurely pace. We retreated to our mobile kennel. The terrier had stopped sulking and was back on the shelf beating the window with his tail. As we drove back to town he showed just how forgiving a Yorkshire terrier can be — a paw was placed gently on my shoulder and my right ear was given an extra sloppy wet lick.

7

The body of an old lady was found lying in her backyard underneath an open bedroom window. Smoke had been seen coming from the house but when the fire brigade arrived the fire had gone out. The initial impression was that the old lady finding her house on fire had panicked and jumped to her death from the window, but this was highly unlikely because the body was naked.

With police swarming all over the house we pieced together what information we could from neighbours and then a formal press conference was called. It was murder — the woman had been raped and thrown from the bedroom window, the fire having presumably been started to cover the crime. The Leeds News Desk was soon on the phone.

'Can you cope or should we send the crime correspondent over?'

'We can cope,' I said not wanting one of our so-called experts from head office trampling all over our patch. Fleet Street however did descend upon us and with them came a feeling of dread. These were the 'big boys' of our profession who would surely expose all our provincial shortcomings. Scotland Yard was called in to assist which created an extra frisson of excitement. This was now a national story.

I did not know what to expect with Scotland Yard. I had been brought up on a diet of old films in which detectives were constantly pursued by a baying mob of journalists. The reporters were treated as if they were only one step up from the villains — a horde that had to be kept at bay with shouts of: 'No comment'. Real life proved to be very different. The Scotland Yard superintendent and his sergeant made us welcome. We were told that we were now all part of a team engaged in a hunt for the killer. The police would keep the public fully informed through us and the public would respond with vital information that would solve the crime. We were treated with the utmost courtesy and respect until the boot print story hit the headlines.

One of the national newspapers got the scoop. Boot prints had been found in the garden, the newspaper crowed exclusively and this would provide a vital clue that could lead to the killer. The wrath of Scotland Yard fell on our collective heads. The hitherto nice superintendent turned nasty and the fluency of his vitriol gave us a clue as to how he had risen to exalted rank; we only caught the edge of the storm — what passed between him and the offending newspaper must have been paint blistering. What would the murderer do when he read the story in the newspaper, he raged? Would he not destroy those incriminating boots! Had we no common sense? Had we no sense of social responsibility?

His tirade provided a good defence when the News Desk demanded to know why we had missed the 'great story' about the boot prints. With fingers crossed we put ourselves on the side of the angels and retorted: 'Scotland Yard did not want that publishing in case the murderer destroyed the evidence. We were being socially responsible.' To which the crisp reply came from the news desk: 'We'll decide when you can be socially responsible.'

A soldier was arrested and charged with murder and thankfully all reporting activity ceased, there was no more competition with unscrupulous national reporters, the case was sub judice. We waited for the assizes and the arrival of a high court judge and the prospect of seeing the grim ritual of someone being sentenced to death.

<h1 style="text-align:center">8</h1>

My two years army service had coincided with a rare period of peace as a dazed world recovered from the slaughter of the Second World War. Then it started all over again. Young National Servicemen were caught up in the Palestine troubles trying to control the number of Jews wanting to return to what they regarded as their homeland in the face of the resident Arabs who regarded the land as theirs and then full scale warfare broke out in Korea in 1950. The communists in the north invaded the south and acting on a United Nations mandate the Americans and ourselves tried to stop them only for it to get worse with the Chinese joining in. I followed these events in far flung parts of the world with some alarm, Thousands of British reservists were being called up including boys who had been at my school and were only a few years younger than myself.

I was briefly called back into the army for what was called Class Z training. It lasted for two weeks and its purpose was to ensure that if we too were needed we would be fully trained, lean fighting machines ready for combat. That fortnight in a tent in Wales however gave me no confidence that this object could be achieved. My growing journalistic scepticism damned the whole enterprise from the start particularly as with two stripes on the arm of my ill-fitting uniform I found myself as a clerk in a heavy anti-aircraft regimental HQ.

I fastened my stripes on my sleeves with safety pins feeling it pointless to do anything more permanent for just fourteen days. When the colonel walked into the marquee which served as his office during the day and my bedroom at night he blinked but said nothing. The sergeant major however was more communicative.

'Bombardier,' he said to me surprisingly politely under the circumstances, 'the colonel sends his compliments and says: 'get those bloody stripes sewn on properly''.

For a fortnight I typed battery orders, printed menus for the officers' mess, wrote letters and supposedly prepared myself for holding off the Chinese hordes sweeping through Korea. Every night I hid the typewriter in a corner of the tent, collapsed my table-cum-desk onto the grass and slept on it. I was the HQ's lonely guard. Every morning before the colonel and the rest of the staff arrived I had rapidly to convert my bedroom back into an office. Thankfully they never caught me in my pyjamas.

Somewhere in the distance we could hear the booming of our regiment's guns — the gun crews were at least doing something worthwhile but my 'training' was typing menus; the cooks were training hard too turning out beans, chips and corn beef. The officers sensed the growing irritation among us belligerent civilians turned soldiers so a treat was organised. We were taken to the firing range down by the sea shore and issued with rifles that must have seen service in the First World War. Five shiny new cartridges, still slippery with grease, were laid in the sand beside us. We were given the order to fire but the sand stuck to the greasy bullets and they refused to go into the breach.

'Fire!' came the order again but much more urgently. There was still no answering fusillade. We took out our handkerchiefs and frantically polished our bullets. I pictured hordes of screaming Chinese rushing towards me. If this were real I was going to die.

The fortnight ended with a parade of troops marching past our regimental marquee and the colonel standing outside taking the salute. One column of men with their heads rigidly turned 'eyes right' deviated from their true path and tripped en masse over the marquee guy ropes. The colonel tactfully retreated back inside until order was restored.

I read later in the newspapers that there were some 80,000 of us Class Z reservists being called up for training. Government policy decreed: *'It is important that these reservists should return to civil life with the feeling that their time had been usefully occupied.'*

On my return to civilian life I felt somewhat different: if we were the army's reserve in time of need then God help us all.

9

The High Court Judges arrived in the city with all the usual pomp and ceremony including fanfares of trumpets; the civic leaders in their robes and finery turned out to meet them. It was another piece of much loved local tradition, an echo of the days when the King sent his judges round the country with orders to open up the jails and dispense justice on all the poor felons who had been rotting there since their Lordships' last visit. We were more interested than usual because we had a murderer on trial for his life.

'Not guilty,' said the thickset young soldier standing in the dock. Scores of faces in the gallery of the packed court room were staring down at him as if from the 'gods' in a theatre. Was this the man who had raped a woman of seventy, thrown her body out of her bedroom window and then tried to set the house on fire? The press box was crammed as the bowing rituals of judge and barristers were concluded and the prosecution opened its case.

'Members of the jury . . .'

It was like a stage play, the judge in his red

robe and full wig and a full public gallery up above. I did the first 'take' of copy and eased my way out of the press bench. From the public telephone outside I started the running story for the evening paper. The barrister was still on his feet when I returned and a colleague tip-toed out through the groaning court door with the second instalment.

I was full of admiration for the dramatic lucidity of Queen's Counsel. We discovered in detail why the police had been so upset about the story of the boot prints; the accused had indeed tried to get rid of them but being a soldier he could not do without boots. Instead he had swapped them with another soldier who was being posted overseas. The police traced this soldier and had taken him off a troop ship in the Mediterranean and flown him back home at great expense to give evidence — no wonder Scotland Yard had been so cross.

After the initial opening excitement the long drawn out process of sanctioning a judicial murder got under way.

★　★　★

As a reporter I had to learn all about the rituals of a very important organisation — the complex workings of the city council. Outwardly this organisation sprang into public life on the first Monday of every month. A small procession would emerge from the front door of the Mansion House, a Georgian residence of doll's house prettiness. The cry would go up: 'Make way for the Right Honourable Lord Mayor!' and if there were people on the pavement, they would stand back reverently.

First came the sword bearer wearing the Cap of Maintenance. As a sceptical young reporter I thought this tradition with his hat a bit silly — a grand version of: 'Yahoo, I'm not taking my cap off for you, so there!' The mace bearer followed, a priceless piece of ancient silverware resting on his shoulder, and finally came the Lord Mayor himself, begowned, feather-hatted and a 17th century gold chain worth a king's ransom about his neck.

Long-serving aldermen and councillors took it in turn to be Lord Mayor and live in the Mansion House with its butler, servants and a Rolls Royce parked around the back. For some of them moving out of a little terrace house on an estate into a stately town house was quite a shock but Bill, the Lord Mayor's butler, made them all welcome and they adapted to the good life with enthusiasm. The Lord Mayor was allowed to choose his Sheriff, so the two men with their spouses had an enviable social life and a waist-threatening year of dinners and dances, receptions and meetings, welcoming important visitors and generally being feted throughout the city. We reporters got to know the Lord Mayors very well indeed because we were on the same work circuit. But for them the good times only lasted a year and then it was back to reality — a shock akin to the Devil telling poor old Faust that his time was up. It was back to the council house and riding on the bus. With malicious glee the local wags would say: 'in this city there is nothing more ex than an ex Lord Mayor'.

Those Monday nights had a sense of occasion about them, for the council was the ticking heart of the city. It was the place where things were decided and because of this the newspapers gave it full coverage. We in the press box felt we were part of the whole democratic process — explaining the debates and the decisions to our readers. At intervals throughout the evening I crept out and phoned copy for the back page lead in tomorrow's newspaper.

In the council chamber, aldermen in their red robes gathered beneath the portraits of former Lord Mayors, their stern gazes reminding everyone what a serious business it all was; the place reeked of authority and history. In one of the adjoining rooms had not the Civil War Parliamentarians handed over a ransom of silver to the Scots in return for the custody of Charles I? The place always gave me mental images of a delegation of hairy, kilted highlanders carefully counting out the coinage into piles on the table to be sure they were not short-changed.

In theory the Lord Mayor was the leader of all the pomp and ceremony on council nights but it was really the Town Clerk who captained the ship. In his wig and gown he sat below the Lord Mayor's 'throne' quietly but knowingly omnipotent.

'Perhaps the Town Clerk would guide us,' the Lord Mayor would murmur when faced with some obscure point of procedure and the bewigged figure would rise and give judgement. We all worked late on those Monday nights.

10

Tension was growing in the court room. The prosecution finished its case and then came a surprise — the prisoner elected not to give evidence. That sent a murmur through the court room and there was a feeling that the rope was coming closer. The defence counsel spoke at length casting doubt on all the evidence but one sensed the die had already been cast. The judge summed up and the jury went out. New barristers shuffled onto the benches. Other cases were brought in for pleas and were quietly dealt with. The atmosphere was subdued, everyone was waiting. In a back room twelve people were deciding if a young man should live or die.

It was mid afternoon during a burglary trial that there was a rustle of activity among those sitting alongside the judge. An usher in court dress complete with black stockings was whispering in the judge's ear. The jury had reached a verdict, the burglary case was suspended and a whisper went round the court complex; the public gallery rapidly filled, rows of faces were looking down on those of us crushed into the well of the court.

We felt we were part of a scene in a stage drama only this was real. The judge had quietly withdrawn as the court room filled up but now he returned.

'All rise!' came the shout and there was a great shuffling of feet as everyone respectfully stood. And now all eyes turned to the young man in the dock. He did not seem at all concerned standing there with his hands on the bar and a large policeman on either side of him. The guilty verdict came as no surprise not even to the accused but the collective intake of breath was clearly audible. A chilling ritual began.

The judge nodded to his attendant who produced what looked like a black lace handkerchief which he placed on the judge's wig. For a moment I had an incongruous memory of granddad on the beach in his deck chair, a crumpled knotted handkerchief on his bald head, but that image vanished as the usher meticulously arranged the four corners of the black cap so it sat in a neat square. The silence while this was going on was stifling — it was like watching some barbaric ritual in a medieval castle. With the black cap in place the words of the death sentence were intoned:

' . . . you will be taken from this place to a place of lawful execution and there you will be hanged by the neck until you are dead. And may God have mercy on your soul.'

Hundreds of death sentences had been delivered in that same court room over the centuries but then the place of lawful execution had been the public gallows in the town. Hangings had been popular public 'entertainments' and even in Victorian times special train excursions brought in the spectators. It felt barbaric that hangings were still going on even though they were no longer a public spectacle. It was the last death sentence pronounced in that ancient court room. The death sentence was repealed and I for one was glad. I did not want to watch that grim ritual ever again or to imagine what followed.

From the soldier in the dock there was little reaction — a purse of the lips and a muttered comment which the police officers said later was: 'Roll on death'.

After the regulatory waiting period death did indeed roll on and the young soldier was hanged.

11

I was experiencing the pangs of ambition. Reporters kept leaving the local paper and taking up jobs in Fleet Street. I saw their by-lines in the national papers and I had longings to follow them. I bought and read the journalists' own journal and applied for jobs on the BBC but never got a reply. Apart from any professional inability I thought I knew why. On application forms there was a section asking for degrees, diplomas and other qualifications. I always had to leave this accusingly blank. The war and my father's constant moving about within the London and North Eastern Railway had all but destroyed my education and that had always left me resentful and frustrated. Meriel and I thought of emigrating and New Zealand appealed until we met a New Zealand journalist travelling England on a scholarship. He was with us for a week.

'Why do you want to leave?' he asked. 'This is a wonderful place to work. If you go to New Zealand you will only catch the national disease'.

'What's that?'

'Apathy,' he said. 'It's endemic. The place is riddled with it'.

I spoke to some of the older reporters who had been in the city all their working lives.

'If you want to go, go now,' they urged me. 'This damn place is the graveyard of ambition.'

So I continued applying fruitlessly for jobs and then quite suddenly Walter the chief reporter announced that he was leaving. He was taking up the post of private secretary to one of the great land-owning Yorkshire lords and we were all very impressed and envious. I spoke to the News Editor at Leeds asking what happened now. As a former captain in the Royal Marines he was brisk and to the point.

'Do you want the job or not?'

'Yes.'

'Well stop messing about. Write to the Editor and tell him you want it and be quick about it.'

There was a need for speed. I met one of the senior reporters from the local paper in the street. He sheepishly showed me a copy of a letter he had written to my Editor; he too wanted the position.

'I didn't want to go behind your back,' he said.

I had a heavy sick feeling as I read the letter.

'If Mr Scott is considered too young for this very important post,' the letter said, 'then I would like to put my name forward.'

'Is that OK?' asked the senior reporter looking genuinely anxious. I could hardly fling myself at his throat in a public place.

'That's it,' I told Meriel. 'He's been here years. He knows the city backwards. He'll get the job, certain of it, and I don't want to work under him!'

A week later a letter arrived from Leeds. It too was brief and to the point.

'You are hereby appointed chief reporter of the York Office of the Yorkshire Post. In order to maintain a differential with other staff your salary will be increased by five shillings a week.' Sir Linton Andrews, Editor.

George the photographer and former bomber pilot did not like it. Someone was being put in charge of the office who had only reached the heights of full corporal during National Service

'Let's get something straight from the start,' he said. 'You do not give me orders. I take my instructions from head office, not from you.'

This was the former officer putting the former NCO in his place.

'OK' I said but it was not that easy. George had a prickly attitude towards everyone and even head office avoided dealing with him directly. Nearly every day over the phone they told me: 'Tell George to do this, or tell him to do that.'

'Why can't you tell him?'

'He's in your office — you tell him,' was always the response.

And the inevitable reaction was: 'Whose stupid, daft idea was that? Did you put them up to this?'

And then there was the problem with transport. Ideas that emanated from George usually involved a car trip out into the country for which he could claim mileage. But if a reporter came up with a story the travel still had to be done in George's car; there was, we were told, a union arrangement — photographers took reporters not the other way round; the picture men had heavy equipment which travelled in the boot of their car. And that was the way it was. The union had spoken.

With my new appointment however my ambitions were temporally satisfied and thoughts of Fleet Street and New Zealand were banished. I was now Chief Reporter responsible for news gathering over a vast swathe of the North Riding and it took a few days before the enormity of all this dawned on me. If anything happened in this area I was supposed to know about it and quickly so the county newspaper could keep its discerning readers informed. I felt very proud and rather important until I overheard a sarcastic comment on my appointment from one of the bright boys at head office.

'Rather like being made captain of a canoe, don't you think?'

Wounding but true I thought and I still did not have a telephone at home. Even an interview with the local telephone manager pleading the needs of my new high position fell on deaf ears. Telephone lines were still rationed so every night someone turned out at 9pm and again at midnight and trudged to the nearest public telephone to call the police and fire brigade to make sure that our part of Yorkshire was not going up in flames. And every day at 4pm there was another routine: 'the list.'

At that hour, without fail, a list of the day's stories and pictures had to be phoned through. It was like one of those endless labours imposed by the Greek gods — poor tormented souls pushing boulders uphill only for them to roll back down again. Every day we filled the 'bucket' with stories and pictures and every morning that bucket came back empty and we started filling it up again. No excuses. Nothing happening? Find something!

Fortunately sleepy, shabby old York that had so depressed me when I returned from National Service was stirring . . . The 1951 Festival of Britain had been a clarion call to the nation to celebrate a new beginning after years of war and York had been chosen as one of the regional cultural centres: that sent a shiver of interest through the city but as ever the focus was not on the future but on the past. The centre piece of the York Festival was a revival of the four hundred year old medieval mystery plays. Every night for three weeks Christ was crucified in the museum gardens before silent reverent crowds and every night came the resurrection and floodlit angels appeared triumphantly in the windows of the ruined abbey that served as a backdrop to the plays. Thereafter the festival was repeated every three years. Everyone in the city was either in the vast cast or making costumes or helping out in some way. The festival brought a buzz to the city that I had never experienced before. Few realised it at the time but a sleepy old town which had traditionally relied on chocolate and the railways for its livelihood was slowly, unwittingly, acquiring a new industry — tourism. Not everyone liked it. Favourite tea-rooms were annoyingly full of strangers. Button badges were popular proclaiming: 'I am not a tourist I live here!'

12

When more senior reporters at head office baulked at assignments they thought a little too physical I was given a chance to shine; that was how I came to be at a local RAF aerodrome in a briefing room with a crowd of American airmen all looking and behaving like extras in a war movie.

The Cold War in Europe kept threatening to get hot so both sides were playing war games to keep each other frightened and alert. Americans and six of their giant flying box-car aircraft had arrived in Yorkshire from Germany on a NATO co-operation exercise. They were to carry a company of British paratroopers into a pretend battle. I noticed however that the aircrew in their leather jackets and flying helmets were not paying much attention to the briefing; they had been told they were going to fly, follow-my-leader, to the dropping zone which was on a moor only twenty miles away; their attitude oozed casual confidence: twenty miles man? No sweat.

I climbed into the last aircraft and the flight sergeant met me and insisted that I wore a parachute — just in case.

'Big doors, lots of draught, don't want to lose you,' he shouted over the noise of the engines. I climbed up a ladder into the cockpit and was fitted with headphones and given a seat behind the pilots. I felt very important sitting there with my parachute and headphones. It was nearing dusk and rain was lashing the windscreen. Behind me the cavern-like body of the flying box-car was filling up with heavily laden figures in khaki.

The aircraft in front of us took off its lights winking as it rose from the end of the runway. We followed with engines roaring and lurched upwards into more rain and cloud. I heard the pilot's voice over the intercom.

'Can you see Charlie five in front?'

'Negative,' came a reply.

'Say again.'

'Negative.'

There was a momentary pause.

'Shit!' said a quiet voice. 'You'd better get the map out and start navigating.'

It was not a good omen. I had a job to do however so as ungainly as a camel with my hump of a parachute on my back I climbed back down the ladder from the flight deck and into the vast interior of the aircraft. I got out my notebook and started interviewing. With the exception of the officers all the soldiers were territorials. The major in charge had fought at Tobruk as had his lieutenant who had a large canvas bag marked 'Danger Explosives'. I eyed it nervously.

'Just a few bangers to make the battle a bit more interesting,' he said.

I moved on to the men sitting in rows in the semi-darkness and did some interviews.

'What's that thing you've got on your back,' one of them said to me while winking at his companion.

'A parachute,' I said. 'The Yanks gave me it.'

Compared with the para's bulky chute mine was a sleek green silk affair with a shiny metal handle to pull.

'Yankee chutes are a load of rubbish,' said another soldier. 'Not a patch on our fixed line jobs.'

'Very dodgy,' said another.

'Have they told you how to use it?' another chipped in.

I knew I was being ribbed but doubts crowded into my mind. Was it true you had to count 'one two three' before you pulled the chord? Suddenly lights were flashing, the air crew were shouting and two great doors at the rear of the box-car were sliding open. The paras were all on their feet, their release lines hooked onto an overhead wire and they were all shuffling towards that gaping void. Someone started singing and everyone joined in:

'Toot, toot tootsie goodbye . . .'

It was all very exciting. The major was at the head of the column and one of the dispatchers had his hand on his shoulder. I didn't envy him leaping out into oblivion. But it did not happen. A red light flashed urgently and the dispatcher pulled the major back while talking animatedly over his intercom. The soldiers were waved back to their seats. The aircraft banked steeply making us all cling on and after a few minutes of steady flight the warning lights started flashing again. Once again the major and his men waited on the brink but this time there were no cheery songs. And once again they were sent back. The dispatchers were whispering among themselves watched by rows of suspicious belligerent eyes in darkly camou-flaged faces. The great doors closed and we were cocooned once again within the aircraft. The major cupped his hands around my ear and shouted above the roar of the engines:

'Can you find out what the Hell is going on?'

I put my notebook back in my pocket and climbed the ladder out of the hold and went up into the cockpit. Someone had indeed found a map but it did not seem to be doing them much good. The two pilots were consulting the paperwork and staring out into the darkness. The pilot beckoned me forward.

'Recognise anything?' he said pointing downwards. I was no aerial navigator and I was astonished when I did look down. We were flying over what appeared to be a vast city giving off a brilliant display of lights, a city far larger than York which should have been the first turning point on the way to the drop zone. I wondered if on reaching York, probably some time ago, they had turned right instead of left. I remembered the aircraft banking sharply in that direction. Clearly they did not know where they were.

'I think that might be Leeds down there,' I shouted, 'or Bradford'.

'Where the Hell is Leeds?'

The navigator consulted his map and there was much muttering on the flight deck. The flight sergeant suggested that I might like to join the paras back in the hold so I took the hint and left.

'What's happening?' the major asked.

'We're lost.'

'Bloody Yanks! Can you imagine what this does to the lads?'

He nodded at the silent rows of men.

'Inter-service co-operation! Bloody typical!'

The pilot never did find the dropping zone but he did find our airfield and we landed to sarcastic cheers from the 'cargo'. Transport was waiting and some very disgruntled paratroopers were launched into battle by lorry. It made a good story the next day. 'Paratroops 'lost' over Yorkshire,' shouted the headlines. Was I giving comfort to the enemy by highlighting military incompetence? Not for the first time I wondered if I had too sensitive a conscience to be a journalist?

13

I was getting to know more of the characters who ran this overgrown village. Our next Lord Mayor was a friend of my father-in-law's — both of them being shrewd Yorkshire businessmen who in their younger days had bought and sold cattle together. Alderman Billy Bridge was just as affable and approachable in his robes of office as when he was stomping around the cattle market in his bowler hat.

'Anything you want to know lad just ask,' he told me and the offer was extended to my friend Stacey a reporter on the local paper. Alderman Bridge was not the most articulate of public speakers at council meetings and he knew it. Getting himself ravelled up in a long sentence during a debate he would stop in exasperation and exclaim: 'Tha' knows what I'm trying to say but if tha' doesn't, the press lads do, so you can read what I meant to say int' papers tomorrow.'

The system seemed to work but often Stacey and I had to seek clarification privately after the meeting. One social benefit of the relationship was his connection with the regional road hauliers association which meant that Meriel and I were always invited to the association's annual dinner and dance. In return I tried to get a good account of the speeches in the newspaper the next day. And then another figure rose to even more prominence — Hans Hess, the curator of the local art gallery. He was bristling with energy, always meticulously dressed with his neat, iron-grey hair cut short. He talked at breakneck speed with a heavy German accent which made him sound fiercely intimidating. The City Fathers who employed him were overawed by his intelligence and frequently silenced by his verbosity. I got on well with Hans who was always good for a quote but the relationship between this foreign intellectual and the City Fathers could be prickly. Hans was a German and in those immediate post-war years hostility towards the Boche ran deep; it mattered little that Hans was Jewish and that his family had fled from the Nazis. He was only too happy to expand on his life story when I interviewed him about some painting the council had grudgingly bought on his advice for the city's art collection. With his feet up on his desk we often had long expansive chats in his office.

'People here will never understand.' he

said. 'For them I am a German. That's it! No good!'

He wagged a finger at me.

'We had a good business in Germany and then Hitler came, the anti-Semitism it grew worse and worse but my father would not leave. 'It will pass,' he said. Our family home was hidden behind a high fence — a good, solid fence, set in concrete, a good German job of a fence. Then we woke up one morning and the fence had gone — every piece of it. We never heard them taking it away. There was nothing between us and the street — nothing. And my father said: 'Now we go!' and we did. And do you know where we go?'

The dramatic, heavily accented voice rose angrily.

'I tell you where we go! To England and into an internment camp for aliens! That's where we go.'

I murmured sympathetically.

'And then we are shipped to Canada,' said Hans, 'chased by U boats across the Atlantic. The English wanted to lock us up and the Germans wanted to drown us. Nobody wanted us.'

'Never mind,' I said. 'You're settled here now.'

Fierce blue eyes were looking at me.

'You think I'm settled? How long do you

think they will put up with me, eh? Telling them what to do — how long? They will find an excuse.'

Hans Hess knew a great deal about the arts and it turned out he could also see into the future.

14

News gathering became a routine. It was a daily round of courts, council meetings, fires, accidents, and formal dinners. Every day we scoured the city meeting people and looking for stories. But the big story was already happening all around us. Old buildings were being pulled down and new ones going up and there were rumblings that it was all happening too fast. There was an outcry when a row of medieval houses in a narrow street disappeared to make way for a row of charmless new shops. Respected figures in the local conservation societies sounded the alarm. The debate dominated the City Council: could conservation and progress go hand in hand? Other historic cities were facing the same problems because of the increasing speed of post-war redevelopment. The government was lobbied and the government listened. The renowned town planner Lord Esher was appointed to study how historic towns could adapt to 20th century living without having their unique character destroyed; our town was chosen for the study.

As Lord Esher set to work the rumours were soon flying. One idea leaked out that was revolutionary and the local trades-people were up in arms. It was a proposal to keep traffic out of the narrow streets completely, to 'pedestrianize' them, which was not only a new idea but also a new word. The shop-keepers cried woe and disaster. I had some sympathy with them for many people from the outlying villages, including my father-in-law, did their city centre shopping by car and their vehicles were dumped anywhere convenient. My father-in-law however took city centre shopping a stage further — he never actually got out of his car. He would drive onto the pavement outside the butchers in the main street and they would come out and serve him through the car window. A slightly different system operated at the bakers. Parking his vintage Rover car on the pavement he would pip his horn and a member of staff would appear in the shop window. Father-in-law would point to the required bread buns and cakes in the window and they would be neatly parcelled up and brought out to him. Lord Esher would have to be careful — new-fangled ideas about banning cars from the city were going to upset a firmly established way of life.

★　★　★

I was becoming obsessed with holes in the ground. They opened up fascinating worlds for me and they were appearing all over the city. Whenever a developer put a spade into the ground he stirred up history in the shape of bones or pots and that brought in the archaeologists buzzing like bees after honey.

Crouched at the bottom of most of these holes I usually found Peter Wenham, a local history lecturer and leader of the Sealed Knot, a Civil War re-enactment group. I had met him on the field of battle leading the charge, waving his sword at the head of a small army, most of whom were girl history students. I met him again on his hands and knees in a huge excavation alongside one of the main roads out of the city. A Romano-British graveyard had been discovered and scores of skeletons lay uncovered and in full public view. People walking by on the busy road stopped to stare and a policeman eventually had to be sent to keep them moving.

Mr Wenham explained to me what had been found: skeletons with pots of food beside them for the afterlife and skeletons with coins in their mouths to pay the ferryman for their journey over the River

Styx. With arms gesticulating he pointed out where the Roman road had been in relation to the graveyard and the town. Peter was an enthusiast and was in full flow but then stopped abruptly. An amateur historian up on the pavement had been explaining in whispers to a friend what the excavation was all about.

'No, no, no,' shouted Peter striding towards him. 'These are not Vikings. These are Romano-British people. The Vikings came much later.'

And from the bottom of his trench he launched into an eloquent history lecture; a crowd soon gathered for the free entertainment. Peter pointed out various skeletons for closer analysis and the sea of faces looking down into the trench grew larger until the crowds parted and a policeman appeared.

'Mr Wenham you must really stop doing this, sir. You are causing an obstruction on the highway. You are going to cause an accident. If you don't stop giving these impromptu lectures, sir, I am going to have to report you. Now! Everybody, move on please.'

Shamefaced, Peter stopped waving his trowel in the air and I got back to my interview. I was reluctant to become too involved in the past but Peter's enthusiasm was infectious. He was my guide around the

Yorkshire battlefields for a series of newspaper articles; he painted vivid word pictures of the civil war battle flags gathering on the crest at Marston Moor and with sweeping arm gestures he would bring the Roundhead cavalry crashing down into the Royalist lines. And at Stamford Bridge he conjured up the Viking hero standing on the bridge and holding back King Harold's army until someone sneaked under the bridge and unsportingly ended the encounter with a nasty upward thrust of a spear.

It was becoming difficult to keep track of all the interesting holes being explored in the city, so much so that a message about a hole being dug in the floor of the cathedral did not arouse much interest.

15

I was given a cat for my birthday. It came in an open topped, gift-wrapped box and was making funny noises as Siamese cats do. A dominant personality entered our home and we had to adapt to her ways, not her to ours. The cat would not sleep in the basket we provided downstairs. Instead it roamed the house until it found the hot water tank in the airing cupboard and claimed that for its abode. Her basket had to be put on a shelf in the cupboard and our sheets moved elsewhere.

To respond to her nightly demands to go hunting I cut a cat flap in the kitchen door and like anxious parents we would lie awake at night waiting for the tell-tale bang of the cat flap opening and signalling her return. There followed padding footsteps on the stairs followed by the athletic bound into her warm bed in the airing cupboard. That damn cat was warmer and more comfortable in our house than we were. And then late one night she jumped onto the bed and dumped a live vole on the bedclothes. The vole gave a pathetic little shriek and Meriel gave a louder one. The vole ran for its life with the cat in pursuit and I pursued the cat. Obviously the cat won, tossing the poor vole triumphantly in the air and playing with it like a ball. I grabbed it and held it trembling in my hands and stalked shivering down the garden in my pyjamas to release the timorous beastie into the field; returning to the house the cat passed me on the stairs with the vole back in her mouth. She waited for me on the landing with a puzzled look on her face which eloquently inquired: 'But I've brought this for you . . . Don't you want it?'

I locked the cat in the lounge and returned the trembling creature to the field while the yowling, frustrated huntress vented her fury on the back of the sofa by ripping the fabric with her claws. And then on one of her nocturnal hunting expeditions my birthday present was killed on the road by a car. And that was that. Perhaps it was time for us to bring something much more important into our lives.

16

I was deeply and enjoyably involved in an article about the latest archaeological find in the city when the telephone rang.

'Gerald Nabarro the MP is at the Station Hotel,' said the man on the news desk. 'He wants to talk to a reporter.'

'When?' I asked.

'Now of course. Nip down there and find out what he wants.'

This was one of life's aggravations — I was always working to someone else's time-table never my own. The outside world always dictated when I should do things. Here we were again having to drop everything to fit in with someone else's time schedule. Nabarro, I was told, would be waiting for me in the hotel lounge and as I strode in there he was in an armchair with a small table in front of him strewn with papers. I recognised him instantly from newspaper photos and cartoons; his huge handlebar moustache was even more flamboyant in real life.

The MP was a charismatic character with a reputation for being a bit of a maverick so much so that the tabloids had nicknamed him the 'abominable showman'. I introduced myself and at close quarters the moustache looked quite preposterous.

'Coffee,' he said snapping his fingers and a waitress appeared far faster than they did whenever I was at the hotel waiting for meetings to finish.

'Good of you to come so quickly,' he said to me affably. 'Get your notebook out.' And he launched into an attack on government secrecy following the result of a recent review of Post Office finances. So what, I thought. Had I left my promising hole-in-the-ground story for this? He must have sensed my lack of excitement for he added: 'And I have it on the best authority that they are planning to increase the price of the first class postage stamp.'

He paused for effect.

'They are going to put it up to sixpence — six pence!'

The moustache quivered with indignation.

As the stamp was currently only four pence this was quite a jump.

'They are going to sneak this in without proper consultation. Think of the extra cost to industry, to business — it's ridiculous, scandalous!'

He watched as I put my Pitman's

shorthand to good use.

'There you are,' he said. 'Exclusive interview. 'Sixpenny stamp on its way,' says Nabarro.''

He drank his coffee and indicated that I should drink mine.

'How long have you been in this game then?' he asked.

The sudden switch to the personal was startling.

'Just a couple of years.'

'Enjoying it?'

I was going through one of my dissatisfied moods so I was honest.

'Not really,' I said.

Eyebrows were raised and I noticed for the first time that they too were generously hairy.

'Surprised at that,' he said. 'Mind you it's a profession that gives very young men like you the self confidence to walk straight up to public figures like me in hotel lounges and chat to them. So I wouldn't knock the job too much.'

He drained his coffee and extended a hand across the table.

'Good luck in your career young man,' he said, which I thought was very decent of him.

My exclusive interview with Nabarro MP made a paragraph on the front page with the sixpenny stamp headline much as he had predicted. I concluded that he probably knew more about my 'game' than I did particularly as my archaeological story was buried on one of the inside pages. I feared I was getting dangerously parochial on my own little patch?

17

We wanted to become parents and that provoked an urge to earn more money and an opportunity to do so arose by chance. Mother-in-law, a staunch supporter of her village's Women's Institute, insisted that I gave a 'little talk' about journalism to her group. It was a nerve-wracking experience but apparently successful because my name was put forward and accepted for the county WI's official speakers' list; thereafter once or twice a week I found myself driving off into the dales trying to find some tiny village and locate its meeting hall in the semi-darkness. I would search for signs of life — lit up windows or a huddle of parked cars indicating a gathering. Sometimes I could navigate the last few hundred yards by the faint strains of female voices singing 'Jerusalem'.

Having located the village hall it was like entering a time capsule of rural life. The door invariably squeaked and groaned as I entered and the singing would waver for an instant all heads would turn. I stepped from darkness into a warm, cosy world inhabited by worthy ladies chattering around tables full of cups, saucers, buttered scones and the entries for the monthly competition.

'Oh good, the speaker has arrived,' was the usual greeting expressed with a tone of relief. One sensed a perennial uncertainty about whether the speaker would make it to their remote community. Sometimes there would just be a stalwart group of seven or eight waiting to be entertained; at other institutes there would be a lively, gossiping gathering of more than twenty. The very small groups were the most intimidating because instead of creating an anonymous audience you became aware of them all as individuals. At one such meeting I tried to avoid eye contact with the well-dressed but very elderly lady sitting stony-faced directly in front of me. I failed to arouse any reaction from her at all and I was surprised when the chair lady whispered: 'Congratulations,' as I sat down.

'When we have a speaker Lady Johnson usually falls asleep,' she said, 'but you kept her awake, well done!'

Other social events were more lively. The annual invitation arrived for the road hauliers' dinner and dance, an event Meriel always looked forward to but this time there was a catch. It was being held in Scarborough which meant a long drive back home in the early hours of the morning. I regretfully declined and Meriel went quiet until a letter arrived from Alderman Bridge. He had booked us into the Grand Hotel for the evening as his personal guests. Meriel was delighted and I was nervous. Was the integrity of the Press under threat here? Was I being bribed? Meriel was annoyed at my hesitation.

'For goodness sake!' she said. 'He's been a friend of my father for years. You don't get all sanctimonious when all those other societies wine and dine you, do you? There's no hesitation then is there?'

She was right of course, but then I spoiled her hopes of a leisurely preparation for an evening out by having to work late at the office. This meant driving to the hotel in evening attire and joining the festivities just as everyone sat down for dinner. We left our suitcase with our next-day clothes at reception and did not even see our room before the festivities began.

'Typical,' Meriel complained.

But the mood soon softened for it was a big glittering affair and the speakers made good 'copy' pungently expressing their fears about government nationalisation plans destroying a 'free' haulage industry. It was only when everyone in their evening dress finery streamed into the ballroom that I saw the dark cloud on the horizon.

'I know, I've seen her,' said Meriel. A woman was wearing Meriel's dress — a long black skirt with the bodice picked out with touches of gold lame. The woman spotted us and even at a distance I could see the shock wave registering. She engaged in urgent conversation with her husband who after some hesitation came towards us. Ignoring me he said to Meriel:

'You are wearing the same dress as my wife.'

Before I could react Meriel replied: 'Indeed I am. Could you compliment your wife on her good taste?'

He was momentarily taken aback but immediately rallied: 'She is very upset. Will you please go and change?'

This was too much. I cleared my throat ready for a manly intervention but Meriel was again ahead of me.

'I'm not driving all the way back to York just to change my dress,' she said.

There was a frosty silence before the husband turned on his heel and walked off. His wife stalked out of the ballroom with him trailing unhappily behind her.

'Stupid woman,' said Meriel. 'I'm not letting her spoil my evening.'

The woman-in-the-same-dress eventually

returned wearing a short skirt and white blouse which made her look ridiculously conspicuous among all the ball gowns. Who else would have noticed and who would have cared? If necessary we could easily have kept to opposite ends of the very large ballroom.

After the last waltz we collected our key and our suitcase from reception and went in search of our room. The ground floor of the Grand Hotel was grand but its standards faded rapidly as one climbed the stairs and we climbed a lot of stairs. First the quality of the carpet deteriorated then the carpet disappeared to be replaced by linoleum. At last we found our room.

We were in one of the turrets that decorated the corners of the huge Victorian building. The room was small and being in a turret it was round and reminded me of a prison cell in a medieval castle. When I saw the fog curling sinuously across the tiny window another image came to mind — Count Dracula's Castle. Out of the tiny window a magnificent view of the harbour was shrouded in mist. I looked down and imagined a fang-toothed creature in evening dress crawling up the stonework towards us. I double checked the window lock before we went to bed.

Lying beside me in the dark Meriel said: 'I don't like this room.'

'Neither do I,' was my response. 'And if anything starts scratching on the window don't let it in. I've left my stake and mallet at home.'

'You stupid man! I won't sleep at all now!'

A deafening noise blasted our ear drums and made the air shake.

'Phoooot!'

Meriel flew into my arms shouting: 'What's that?' The noise stopped and then roared out again. It was a fog horn which sounded as if it were fastened to the wall of our cell rather than to the lighthouse down in the harbour. It blasted away intermittently all night.

18

Meriel was pregnant and wanted to increase the family income in addition to her part-time job at a leisure goods shop in town. On Saturday afternoons a sports reporter from Leeds did 'running reports' on our local football team and Meriel became his telephonist. At fifteen minute intervals the telephone in the press box would ring and Meriel would dictate the scribbled reports to a waiting copy-taker. Fans could read a detailed report on the game that same evening and often a report on the first half would be on sale in the evening newspaper sold outside the club gates as the fans left the ground.

Some reporters wrote and telephoned at the same time but the status of Tom, this particular journalist, was such that he required a reader. In the Press Box too was Noel Blenkin, our war hero, loudly giving his views on team selection as the game kicked off.

'Lord knows why they pick Fenton,' he moaned as one important game started. 'The man is absolutely useless. Look at the silly beggar chasing that ball now. Absolutely useless! My God — he's scored!'

Meriel turned up for duty in the cramped, scruffy Press Box wearing high heels and her best beaver-lamb fur coat and for this she was paid five shillings a match all of which went into a special savings tin for baby clothes.

★ ★ ★

Another festival was being planned and the German born curator at the Art Gallery, Hans Hess, was appointed festival director. This was widely thought to be a curious choice by the City Fathers but in fact the down-to-earth councillors had decided that they preferred the artistic devil they knew rather than some artistic devil from the south whom they knew not. For a time the rumblings of unease were kept behind the scenes. We reporters were more concerned about what famous actors would play Christ and the Devil in the medieval mystery plays and we also interviewed a shy Quaker school girl who was to play the Virgin Mary. Her name was Judi Dench and she said she was hoping to become a professional actress. We wished her luck. Meanwhile we were all borne along by the excitement of the coming event, heralds in medieval costume would be going through the streets, and there would be concerts in the Minster and a Georgian Ball in the Assembly Rooms.

It was the ball that gave the first outward sign that all was not well. Successful attempts had been made to interest and involve the descendants of the rich aristocrats whose subscriptions had built the Assembly Rooms in Georgian times. It therefore became an event which in public minds had been taken over by the local aristocracy. Letters soon appeared in the newspapers that it was an elitist event and the festival director's reaction did not help. If the general public wanted a spectacle, he said, they could have one. He announced that all taxis and 'carriages' would disgorge their costumed and bewigged revellers some distance from the Assembly Rooms. They would then walk to the Rooms acknowledging the applause from admiring spectators lining the pavements.

To many this smacked of Marie Antoinette tossing cake to the peasants while en route to a party at Versailles. The rumblings grew louder when worthy local amateur dramatic groups were refused financial support for their own special festival productions.

'Whose festival is this?' one alderman complained to me in the street. 'It's all arty-farty nonsense with him in charge. And who's this fellow Brecht? Never heard of him! Some German I bet? What's the matter with J B Priestley if you want a good play? And if you want music — what's the matter with a good Yorkshire brass band? And what the 'ell are the Monte Verdi Vespers when they're at home?'

I had to confess that I did not know either but then I did not regard myself as an expert in such matters. I did however think it worthwhile to go and see Hans as a friend and put the rumblings to him. The small, iron-grey-haired little man behind his large desk was quite frightening when angry.

'What is a Festival?' he shouted at me. 'What is it?'

Fortunately he did not want a reply.

'I'll tell you what a festival is. It is a special event, a grand occasion, a time when you put on show the best, the unique, the outstanding. And that costs money. But what do they want? They want me to fritter all the money away on holidays-at-home entertainments, amateur theatricals. Well I won't — that is not a festival! What I am presenting is a festival — a Festival of the Arts. Elitist? Of course it is damn well elitist!'

I tentatively suggested that he was ruffling the feathers of the golden goose, the ratepayers, who were after all providing the cash for this event. Steel blue eyes bored into mine.

'There are people in this city trying to kill this festival — kill it, stone dead!'

Until then this had been a friendly off-the-record chat between two people I liked to think trusted one another but this was now getting serious. I was after all a reporter.

'Are you saying that out loud?' I asked.

Hans hesitated.

'No but you can say it out loud and with my blessing.'

'I can't do that.'

'Why not? You are a respected journalist on an important newspaper. Tell them! Tell them there are people intent on killing this festival!'

'I'm just a reporter,' I said. 'You say it, or get someone else to say it and I'll report it.'

I was flattered. Hans was equating me with some powerful columnist who could express his own opinion. I took out my notebook and held a pencil aloft.

'Can we start again?' I asked.

Hans pursed his lips, thought for a moment and then said it all again while I made a careful shorthand note. He did not criticise JB Priestley, Yorkshire brass bands or the local amateurs but he insisted on his interpretation of a festival as a specialist event. It made headline news next morning and within the City Council emergency meetings were called behind closed doors. I had stirred up a hornets' nest.

At home Meriel had returned from her check-up at the doctors.

'Is everything all right?'

'Sort of,' she said.

The baby was the wrong way round and would not be turned. I discovered all the baby clothes that we had bought had been wrapped up again and put back in their boxes and stored in a cupboard. I asked why.

'We won't be needing them,' said Meriel. I told her not to be so silly.

19

Rumours flew around the Guildhall: Hans Hess and the chairman of the festival committee had resigned; the festival was in crisis. A battle was going on within the festival committee which included a number of highly respected outsiders brought in for their artistic knowledge. Eventually the press was called to the council chamber to hear a statement from the Town Clerk. He wore his formal gown for the occasion so we knew it was serious. The artistic director, Hans Hess he said, had been given a vote of confidence by the festival committee and would be staying on. The Town Clerk would not give the voting figures even though we pressed him but, he added, a number of councillors on the committee had subsequently resigned; the important thing was that the festival would continue. I sneaked round to the Art Gallery to see Hans and found him subdued.

'You won,' I said.

He shrugged his shoulders.

'I have won a battle but lost the war,' he said dramatically. 'They won't forgive me for this . . .'

But I had other things to worry about. Meriel went into hospital. In the strangely empty house I unpacked some of the baby things and tried to familiarise myself with nappy folding. I didn't want to be caught unprepared when they both came home. The news came by telephone. The baby was still-born. I was numb with shock but Meriel was frighteningly calm, so calm that I feared there might be some terrible reaction later.

'I'm fine,' she said. 'I knew things were wrong. I did my grieving well in advance. I'll be alright.'

In fact it was she who carried me though the next few weeks until I came to terms with the fact that I was not a father and I did not have a son. Everyone was sympathetic but what could they say? Life went on. Perhaps we should try again? Work was a diversion until the raw emotions hardened.

20

Gracie Fields was appearing in a concert. 'Our Gracie' was famous — the Lancashire lass who had kept everyone cheerful during the war singing comic songs and sparkling her way through a string of patriotic films. She was a star. Everyone loved her and all the concert tickets had long since been sold out. A crowd turned out to meet her at the railway station. There was a heaving crush and the police had to force a way through for her. We reporters trailed in her wake. The traffic was stopped as she crossed the road into the Station Hotel the crowd surging behind her. Gracie was talking animatedly to her manager in what I thought was quite a posh voice. When she reached the entrance of the hotel the crowd was even larger and I heard her demanding: 'Get me a chair! Get me a chair!' A bell boy brought one and in seconds she was standing on it facing the crowd with her arms outstretched.

'Eeh it's lovely to see you,' she shouted in the broadest of Lancastrian accents. 'That's the hottest welcome I've had since my Blackpool landlady put curry powder in me coffee instead of brown sugar.'

There was a roar of laughter and she was off cracking jokes. Ten minutes later with everyone still cheering she was helped down from the chair by her manager.

'OK? she asked.

'OK,' he said.

With her fans cheerfully dispersing the great entertainer swept into the hotel.

'You are lucky,' Meriel said to me when I regaled her with all the details. 'You get to meet all the interesting people.'

And she was right. Sophia Loren was making a film in a stately home near the city and Keith in the office was enrolled as an extra. A tall good-looking young man he appeared as an air force officer in a ball-room scene. He waxed lyrical about Miss Loren, who at that time was regarded as one of the most beautiful women in the world; so I went to meet her when a press conference was arranged.

The film was in flashback with her character recalling her marriage into the English aristocracy. Unfortunately her reminiscing was being carried out as she appeared on her eighty-fourth birthday. They had sent a make-up man from London to make a beautiful woman look old and he had succeeded horribly; poor Sophia even had gnarled arthritic hands for the close-ups. We were polite and circumspect but we all ended up interviewing the make-up man; he was a far better story than Miss Loren looking like that.

'She might be glamorous now,' I told Meriel. 'But I know what she's going to look like when she's eight-four and it is not a pretty sight.'

★ ★ ★

I got to interview all the archbishops when they took office and, like the Lord Mayors, we got to know each other reasonably well through the rounds of meetings and events that followed. Relationships varied. My first primate was a distant figure who had an arms-length but highly effective way of acquiring press coverage. His secretary would telephone and say there could be something interesting in his Grace's sermon the next day at some distant village church. I would turn up, pencil sharpened, sitting in the front pew and drawing curious glances from the regular churchgoers. What is he doing here?

His Grace would take the text for the day and learnedly expound its meaning. My mind would wander and then there would be a sharp cough. Keen eyes in an old wrinkled face framed by a shock of white were boring into mine. I picked up my pencil, yes your Grace, I am awake and paying attention.

'Concerning the ethical dilemma facing the church over the atomic bomb . . . '

My pencil flew across the pages.

'Our Christian approach should be . . . '

What followed was beautifully phrased, succinct and newsworthy. There were brief pauses which lasted until my pencil had caught up. The Archbishop then smoothly wove his thoughts on the atomic bomb back into the relevance of the text. Once again quietly and without fuss he had made the front page of the newspaper.

My admiration for our archbishops grew and I was not surprised when one of them was 'translated' to Canterbury. We all felt quite proud using that word — translated — it showed our knowledge of high church language. We knew for instance that our archbishop was Primate of England while the 'other one' who lived somewhere down south was Primate of All England. In those days it was important to know such things.

I was however stunned when television cameras appeared at one press conference and I was told that I was doing the television interview; the proper interviewer was stranded somewhere in a broken-down car and I was standing in for him.

Those cameras with their big fish eyes were intimidating and the floodlights were terrifying. I was in no state for probing questions into the burning issues facing the church even if I had known what issues were burning particularly well at that time, so I cheated.

'Your Grace,' I whispered. 'Would you mind if I asked what your priorities will be when you get to Canterbury.' He nodded his head vigorously

'And then perhaps how you have enjoyed your stay up here . . . ?'

More vigorous nods. The lights came on and the cameras turned.

'Your Grace,' I said. 'What will be your priorities when you arrive in Canterbury . . . ?'

And he was off, hands waving, eyes sparkling, the consummate TV performer. As he talked and talked I tried to look serious and intelligent.

'Cut!' someone shouted as the Archbishop eventually drew breath. 'Great! That's all we need.' I never got a chance to ask my second question.

'I'm going to be on the tele,' I gleefully told Meriel and everyone else I happened to meet or accidentally talk to on that day. And the Archbishop duly appeared animatedly talking about what he was going to do in Canterbury. But what of me the dynamic interviewer? There was the back of my head and from me came a low murmuring voice saying repeatedly: 'Yes your grace, no your grace . . . '

21

Lord Esher announced that he had concluded his inquiry into how an ancient city could modernise without destroying its character. The City Fathers, sensing controversy, demanded an advance briefing and it was reluctantly granted on condition that there was no press coverage. The newspapers protested in vain.

'No comment,' was the universal response as the councillors streamed tight-lipped out of the briefing. But next day we received a phone call.

'You know who I am,' said a familiar voice. 'I want to see you, you and that other press lad.'

So we had our own secret meeting and learned all about Lord Esher's plans for traffic exclusion, pedestrian streets and crumbling city centre property being turned into town-houses.

'It's appalling,' said our informant. 'People won't give up their cars. It'll kill the city centre. Absolute madness.'

The story made headlines but the uproar was on two fronts — not just at what was being suggested but also about how the story had 'escaped' into the public domain. This was a Government commissioned report and there was even talk of a question being asked in the House of Commons about the 'leakage'. We feared thumb-screws and the rack with our feeble cries of: 'We never divulge our sources of information!' going unheard.

A witch-hunt swept through the city council — who had talked? All the staff who had handled the only typed copy of the report were under suspicion and in danger of losing their jobs. We felt horribly guilty. When quizzed by a senior council official I swallowed hard and made a personal decision — I assured him that no employee of the council was responsible.

That narrowed the suspects down to the aldermen and councillors and they, I felt, could defend themselves; I did not want the sacking of some poor innocent clerk on my conscience. The Town Clerk called off the hunt and the Fourth Estate never did reveal the source of its information. All that happened was the general public got to know Lord Esher's plans a little earlier than expected. The age of deference was passing into history.

22

We were into the Swinging Sixties and Prime Minister Macmillan had told us that we had 'never had it so good'. He also said there was a 'wind of change' blowing in South Africa but I was far more concerned about other things. Meriel was pregnant again and there was another big event brewing. A local girl was getting married. The ceremony was to be in the Minster and was rather special because the groom-to-be was the Duke of Kent; the bride-to-be was Katherine Worsley from Hovingham. The Minster was filled with flowers for the White Rose wedding and our feature writers from head office took over the event much to our annoyance. I pleaded for a role and was told that I could cover the 'procession' after the ceremony. And thank you very much I thought but when the paperwork and the press briefings arrived I realized that it might not be such a poor assignment after all. Hundreds of guests including most of the extended royal family would be attending and they all had to be transported from the Minster to the reception at Hovingham, the bride's home, some miles out in the country. And I was to be part of that procession of cars.

The Minster bells rang, normal city life stopped and the narrow streets were packed with people. Many had slept out all night on the pavements cooking sausages for their supper over camping stoves. It was the first Royal wedding in the cathedral for 633 years — no wonder the world was watching.

With a Royal Press Pass dangling from my lapel I reported to the police officers guarding Dean's Park behind the cathedral; it was here where the Rolls Royce and Bentleys were drawn up in showroom splendour, rows of them with peaked-capped chauffeurs in attendance.

I had been given a number and found I had been allocated a Bentley; the chauffeur deferentially opened the door for me. Already sitting inside was a resplendent figure in a formal morning suit. He introduced himself grandly as representing the Press Association in London and I hated him: what a show-off, dressed up like that just for a ride in a car . . .

We waited completely isolated from the big event going on inside the cathedral so near and yet so far. A whispered jungle telegraph through the chauffeurs kept us informed of the different arrivals; a burst of wild cheering, 'that's the Queen' came the whispers. Even wilder cheering: 'the bride's arrived.' We saw none of them and we sat in silence as the service got under way. At long last there was a stirring of cars near the exit gate and the cheering started up again

The Press Association representative solemnly noted the time in his notebook. Not to be outdone I did the same. The cars shuffled up to the gate and we could at last see the Great West door standing wide open and the red carpet laid down the steps. The Rolls Royce in front of us moved forward and we followed but at the gate we were kept well back. The Queen Mother came down the cathedral steps and the crowd went mad. She stood there for a moment waving before getting into her car and moving off. We were beckoned forward but drove straight past the red carpet. I squirmed round in my seat and looked back. Princess Margaret was coming down the steps and moving towards the open door of the Rolls Royce behind us.

An incredulous thought struck me. On some list buried deep in Whitehall my name came between the Queen Mother and Princess Margaret. But now I was seeing life as *they* saw it on an almost daily basis and it was unnerving. The streets of the city were narrow and a sea of faces was going by only a few feet from the car windows, all kinds of faces, all excited and mouths open, cheering and shouting, lots of little flags waving.

They were going wild at the sight of the Queen Mother ahead of us. A complete frenzy of waving and shouting rippled along the crowd ahead of us. You could lip-read the cries: 'It's the Queen Mother! Isn't she lovely! Yoo hoo!'

And then as we moved slowly by all eyes turned on us . . . The shouting did a dying swoop. Joy was replaced by puzzlement. Fingers were pointed, mouths opened again. A universal murmur could be read on all lips: 'Who are they?'

The Press Association representative rose to the occasion, waving graciously and advising me to do the same.

'No madam,' he said as he waved, 'The gentleman with the moustache is not Prince Paul of Greece.'

He was referring to me of course but fortunately the window was wound up tight. The procession drove on through villages where all the inhabitants had turned out to wave, even in open country there were groups picnicking on the road-side waiting to catch a glimpse of royalty going by. The Press Association representative made an announcement.

'This is the intro to my piece and it is hereby copyright: 'It was cheers comma cheers all the way . . . ''

I hated him even more because I had been thinking along the same lines. At Hovingham the village was en fete. Everyone was out waving. The Worsley family had lived here since the middle ages and this was their 'young Miss Katherine from t'all' who was getting wed.

The cars ahead of us drove through the main gates to where the wedding banquet awaited but our driver swerved to one side and our Royal journey ended in a car park. My part in the grand occasion was over and I never even saw the bride.

But the aftermath lingered for quite a while . . . Even months later I met people who after staring at me for some time suddenly exclaimed: 'I saw you in the royal bridal procession!' and I would modestly confess that I had indeed been there. They had worked out who I was. I was either a Buckingham Palace equerry or a Scotland Yard detective. No-one guessed that I was just a reporter going along for the ride.

23

One month later our daughter was born. Because of the death of our first child, the birth had been a fraught time for both of us but the hospital assured me that all was well. I dashed out of the office in my lunch hour to bring them both home — Meriel and a tiny fragment of humanity fast asleep in a carry-cot.

I made sure the fire was lit and the house was warm for they had both spent the last few days in a centrally heated hospital. Even so Meriel announced: 'It's freezing in here.' I showed her the fresh milk in the fridge and the food I had bought in before putting my coat back on.

'You're not leaving me?' she cried.

'I've got to get back to work'

There was a look of alarm on her face which puzzled me. I honestly thought that women knew all about babies — it was one of their many natural inbuilt talents. I soon realised it was not that simple. We had a demanding little human being on our hands and we were over-anxious parents ill-equipped for the task. And then just as life was achieving normality we decided to move house, or rather it was decided for us. My parents-in-law retired and built a house on a large plot of land in their village; we were offered half the site free. Rumbling ambition was thwarted once again. Now I not only had a daughter to bring up but a new house that required cupboards and curtains fixing. Fleet Street would have to wait yet again.

★　★　★

The Sixties went on 'swinging' although we were not aware of the phenomena. My concession to the new youth-orientated decade was to grow my hair long and wear flare trousers. It was the fashion. Meriel sported white 'kinky boots'. Photographer George made no concessions to the decade's youth culture at all. Sent to cover a blaring open air pop concert he walked amongst the yelling youngsters with huge wads of cotton wool stuck in his ears. Birth control pills were available on the NHS which Meriel was convinced would bring an end to morality as we knew it. Moral attitudes were certainly changing. A judge decided that the book 'Lady Chatterley's Lover' was not obscene after all and 200,000 copies of it were sold in one day. One of them was bought by Meriel who, along with hundreds of others, had ordered it from W H Smiths. She sidled up to the very busy front counter and whispered: 'Mrs Scott. I've ordered a copy.' The overworked, harassed assistant shouted down the length of the shop. 'Mrs Scott's come for her copy of Lady Chatterley!'

Meriel read the book and pronounced it boring; she was more interested in the wedding of Princess Margaret — the first Royal wedding to be televised. Yes I suppose things were 'swinging' but what with a lively daughter and a new house to decorate and cupboards to build we did not feel part of a free, swinging, liberating movement. Once again my age group was out of step with the times — a school boy during the war and a soldier when the world was at peace; now a working man when the young were swinging. For me, every day, that news 'bucket' still had to be filled with the minutiae of local life. There was for instance something suspicious about that hole in the floor of the Minster; people were very wary about talking about it. The stone flags around the base of one of the columns supporting the central tower had been taken up with the intention it was said of relaying them more evenly. But having taken up the flags a large hole had been dug and working at the bottom of it was the donnish figure of an archaeologist from the regional branch of the Historical Monuments Commission. He explained that they were taking the opportunity to find traces of earlier churches on the same site.

'But why have they dug so deep if they are just replacing the flooring?' I asked.

'You'll have to ask them that' — 'them' being the Minster authorities. The archaeologist gave me a learned account of previous churches built on the site all erected, he said, on top of a Roman city. At the mention of Romans my ears pricked up, but then I noticed some fine cracks in the stonework of the column; across them had been laid small pieces of glass held on either side of the crack with dabs of adhesive.

'What are they for?' I asked.

'Not the faintest idea,' said the archaeologist irritated by the interruption of his history lesson.

'We are standing on top of the town's Roman forum. Some of it could still be down there. Only a few more feet perhaps.'

He waggled his trowel at the intervening earth clearly wishing he could sweep it all away and bring the Roman city back to life. I did not pursue the question of those little pieces of glass. Back in the office George was on the rampage.

'Are you coming?' he demanded.

'Where?'

'They want a snow picture.'

It was lying thick and crisp over most of North Yorkshire.

'You don't need me to take a snow picture.'

'We could rescue a cut off village.'

'If it's cut off how do we get in to rescue it?'

'I've got snow chains and we could walk the last bit. I'm going. Are you coming?'

This was blackmail. George was not above sending his pictures through with the briefest of captions but adding the words: 'Story from York Office.' So I collected winter clothing from home and we went slithering down country roads with the expedition seeming more stupid by the minute. Why did George have to include me in his crew?

The weather reports were right. The aptly named village of Cold Kirby was indeed cut off. George carefully drove the car into a snow drift that blocked the road, took a photograph of me pushing it and then carefully reversed the car out again. Not too far away was a farm-house and buildings on the edge of the village. In Wellington boots, scarves and hats we tramped through the snow and hammered on the farmhouse door. The farmer answered.

'We're from the Yorkshire Post,' I announced proudly. 'Come to see how you are getting on.' I could not bring myself to claim that we were rescuing them.

If the farmer was grateful for our concern he kept it well under control but he invited us in. His wife was much more impressed and put the kettle on immediately and made us tea. The mood in the warm farmhouse kitchen was one of incredulity: why had we bothered to come?

'Are you running out of food?' I asked.

'Good heavens no, luv,' said the farmer's wife. 'We could last for weeks and snow never lasts that long here. We're missing the post like. Van can't get through.'

This I decided was going to be a story of Yorkshire grit and endurance in adversity. But I was looking at my watch. Deadlines were approaching and darkness was not far off. I had no wish to be stranded in Cold Kirby however well stocked the larder.

'We'd better be getting back,' I said.

'How did you get in?' asked the farmer. 'I didn't see a car.'

I explained how we had walked the last part.

'Oh you poor dears,' said the farmer's wife. 'No-one walks in this weather. Edward, get the tractor out and take them back to their car.'

So we rode out of cold, cut-off, Cold Kirby on the farmer's tractor. My article about Yorkshire grit and endurance (with pictures) became a 'first into . . . ' story. The excitement of getting a front page by-line put the Minster and its little pieces of glass quite out of my mind.

24

Winter meant the dinner season was upon us, a time when I felt sorry for the Lord Mayor for he had to attend as many as three such functions a week; 'we' the local reporters joined him at most of them and we grew fat together. This urge for feasting was probably a reaction to the rationing of the war years. All the ancient guilds and societies in the city had their annual dinners and they invited each other to dine in a seemingly endless social round. The most prestigious was the Gimcrack Dinner when the country's racing aristocracy wined and dined the winner of the Gimcrack Stakes. This was a glittering, colourful affair with tall hunting aristocrats in their red jackets mingling with rich owners, famous trainers and diminutive jockeys. Before each guest at the horseshoe-shaped table was always a semicircle of wine glasses into which a different drink was poured to complement the near constant stream of courses that appeared. One's shorthand skills risked becoming seriously impaired particularly as lengthy reports on the speeches were expected that night. It was churlish however to wave away eager wine waiters so sly tactics were adopted. With our neighbours' willing help we surreptitiously exchanged our full glasses for their empty ones and remained sober.

While still very junior in the office I had claimed on expenses for the hire of a dinner suit to go to one very formal function. I received a sharp letter from the Editor saying that he expected all his staff to have their own dinner suits; I could however claim three shillings and six pence expenses for laundering a dress shirt. Five shillings could also be claimed for 'returning hospitality.' Suitably humbled I bought myself an evening suit and felt I had moved up in society.

In one season I went to more dinners than most people attended in a life-time and entered a close-knit world of the local great and good. We saw more and more of Bill, the Lord Mayor's butler. At formal functions he would sweep past us in full butler mode and top up our wine glasses in one sweeping motion as he glided by.

'With the compliments of the Lord Mayor,' he would murmur, greatly impressing our fellow diners.

We young reporters became the connoisseurs of the city's dining scene and of its after-dinner speakers. We regularly met the most popular ones who dined out on their wit and eloquence but while it was the professional eloquence of barristers and lawyers that usually kept dinner guests amused there were surprises.

One lady Lord Mayor forced into speech-making by the duties of her office proved such a hit that she went onto the talk circuit when she retired. At her first dinner she had a speech written-out for her by the Town Clerk and we were present when a loquacious butterfly emerged from its dull chrysalis. After carefully reading from her set script and with people dozing over their coffee she suddenly dumped her notes on the table.

'Oh this is so boring,' she said. 'Look I'll tell you what it's like living in the Mansion House, shall I? You know — having a butler and a chauffeur and servants an' all? Would you like to hear about that?'

There were surprised murmurs of agreement and she promptly launched into a hilarious account of her dramatic elevation from housewife to Lord Mayor. She soon had everyone chuckling but when the hilarity was at its height she stopped guiltily and hastily picked up her discarded script.

'The Town Clerk will kill me if I don't tell you this bit.'

And she was serious again but not for long.

She was soon abandoning her notes and revealing even more of the secret life of the housewife turned civic leader. By the end of her year in office she had honed her after dinner speeches into the best in town.

It was after these late night dinners that I met the late duty copy-takers at head office. The paper took copy by phone until midnight so accounts of the previous night's dinners could be read over the breakfast table. During ordinary working hours the copy-takers were bright, friendly ladies who greeted you with a cheery: 'What have you for us today then, luv?' And their fingers would fly over the typewriter keys faster than you could think. But at night it was different. Often we were dictating hesitantly straight from our note-books to someone who sounded like a world weary, retired headmaster. Any pause for thought was greeted with: 'Is that it?' And then the crushing question in a tired bored tone: 'Is there much more of this?'

25

Mother and father had the wanderlust and I was not surprised when in retirement they rented a house in Pwllheli. For mother every expedition into town was a social occasion, involving chats in Welsh on street corners with her many relatives and even longer conversations over shop counters. It was father I felt sorry for because I remembered being there myself during the war standing mutely by my mother's side as that foreign language flowed over me.

'Ydy e'n siarad Cymraeg?' someone would say (Does he speak Welsh?) And they would all look down at me. Mother would shake her head and in English someone might ask how old I was before they lost interest and that lilting, incomprehensible language took over again. I imaged my poor father, a Tyneside Geordie having to endure the same sense of social isolation, but from their letters I learned that he had joined a bowling club and at least knew how to keep the score in Welsh. We were invited for a holiday and I was determined not to let sad old memories undermine my emotions.

My parents' new house was large and gloomy and half buried in an overgrown garden. Daughter Penny appeared subdued in its cavernous rooms with the dark paintings on the walls of Snowdonia in the rain. I feared Welsh melancholy might affect her too but the promise of the beach cheered her up and the sun shining on a blue sea. After a while even the house seemed less gloomy except for that clock on the mantelpiece. Every hour it struck the full Westminster chimes with painful infuriating slowness. And after an interminable pause the hour was struck like a mournful death knell. My emotions were under attack again by a damn clock! What was it about this place? We are on holiday I told myself, enjoy yourself.

I took Penny up the Garn, the little mountain behind the town with dad following on behind slowly and smoking his pipe. The Garn was more of a hill than a mountain, small escarpments of rocks peeping through the grass and bracken presenting an easy walk to the top. Penny sat on the little concrete pillar that held the Ordnance Survey plate and we surveyed the world. To the south was the town and the harbour with the railway line meandering away along the coast before fading out of sight as it made its way towards a horizon dominated by the shape of distant mountains. And to the north were much closer mountains fringing another shore that we could not see. And between us and the mountains lay peaceful stone-walled fields and grazing sheep.

Father and I looked at the mountains and our thoughts collided. I was a young school boy when he visited mother and me in our exile here during the war, and we had walked up all of those. I pointed them out to Penny giving them all names. I discovered that the family gatherings were still going on in the gas-lit parlour behind my Great Uncle Bob's bread shop. To my grown-up eyes the room seemed even smaller now, dark, cramped and gloomy with its black-leaded fire range and a glass-fronted showcase bulging with knick-knacks that looked as if they had lain there undisturbed for centuries. My aunts would sit there in the same tired old armchairs while Great Uncle Bob silently ate at the table in the corner.

Re-visiting the family gathering brought it all back particularly hearing that strange tongue which I could not understand coming from my mother's lips. Nothing had changed since I was a boy. The bell on the spring on the front door still rang for a late customer and Aunt Katie would drift away into the tiny front-room shop with its battered wooden serving counter. As long as there was bread on the shelves the shop was open to sell. Meriel was subdued when we left Auntie Katie's.

'How can she live like that?' she said.

How indeed. It was a sad story. When a young girl Katie had fallen in love with a sailor but the family disapproved so she never married. The rest of her life was spent looking after a tiny shop and keeping house for her brother Bob the baker. The ritual of her life had been set: selling bread from the front room of her house, chapel on Sundays and the nightly visit of her sister Nell. But we escaped to the beach and into the sunshine — we were on holiday. We watched the cormorants diving for fish in the harbour and tried to guess where they would bob back up again and every day we had tea in the same cafe in the high street, carefully choosing a cake from the vast array on offer in the front shop. But always on such holiday visits a small dark cloud lurked on the horizon. Hesitantly mother would ask: 'John, do you think you could take me up to Deugorn Denio. I like to make sure things are tidy.'

Deugorn Denio was the town graveyard, a peaceful place lying snugly at the foot of the Garn, but it always tore my morbid half-Welsh soul to pieces. During the war mother often took me there to change the flowers and to point out the names of ancient relatives including my grandmother. The visits became a family ritual and on these holidays they were resumed. Mother and I would walk between the rows of gravestones with the Garn looking down on us and only birdsong breaking the silence. She brought some flowers and asked me to put them on the family grave. I suppose she wanted it to be a token to a grandmother who died so young that her only grandson never knew her. I wondered what other thoughts mother was thinking as she made things tidy around the grave but they soon became clear. Without turning to face me she said quite briskly: 'You do know of course that I want to come here too . . .'

And after a hesitation she added: 'And so does your dad?'

'Yes, of course,' I said and I looked up at the top of the Garn and tried unsuccessfully to rebuild my feeble emotional barriers. With disturbing clarity I knew why Deugorn Denio had such an effect on me and it was not because it was so calm and peaceful and full of dead people, it was something else; it was because the damn place seemed to be waiting.

When we got back to the house I made

some excuse and went for a long walk by myself and Meriel gave me a long hard look when I returned. There was no need for words. This, I told myself sternly, was ridiculous. The holidays passed and we packed to go home. I had another life to live in a different world. We told Auntie Katie the time we would be leaving and she was outside the bread shop to wave us goodbye looking even more frail and wraith-like. There was silence in the car for a long time.

'You really must . . . ' began Meriel but I interrupted her.

'I know and I will,' I said. 'Just let me get away from those damn hills.'

<h1 style="text-align:center">26</h1>

National events intruded into our world. Enoch Powell made his 'rivers of blood' speech in 1968 causing divisive outcries throughout the country about immigration and racism. Right wing students at our recently founded university caused consternation by inviting him to come and speak. Protest marches and much banner waving followed: 'Freedom of Speech!' 'No Platform for Racism!'

Students in our new university had so far shown themselves to be a very circumspect lot, not ones to cause mayhem, while over in Paris the student disturbances were filling the television screens with tear gas, riot police and rampaging youths. It was all heady infectious stuff for our young intellectuals. Perhaps they too could change the world?

On one student protest I had been told to infiltrate the throng and experience at first hand the reaction of the local police to this new phenomenon — the students were after all not much younger than I was. Despite my disguise of jeans and sweater I was soon spotted; the scruffy, banner waving student next to me spoke in surprisingly cultured tones: 'Awfully glad to have your support in this dispute, sir,' he said.

So much for me being under cover. The police did pounce on that occasion as soon as the protesters tried to halt outside the army recruiting office. I escaped capture but several students appeared in court for obstructing the highway. The magistrates smiled benignly on them and they were let off with a caution. Emotions, however, were not so benign when Mr Powell was involved. Janet, the girl student from the right wing group who had invited him to speak on Keynesian economics was enjoying her moment of fame; we were in constant touch with her as the day grew closer. A room on the university campus had been hired for the meeting, notices and placards sprang up all around town only to be quickly defaced. Spokespersons for both sides appeared giving press conferences. There was a whiff of gunpowder in the air.

I attended the meeting on campus. The hall was bulging with excited students and more kept arriving to pack the stairs and fill the gangways. Flags were waving and there was shouting and chanting. Janet sidled up to the little group of reporters.

'Enoch's here,' she whispered to us, 'but the Registrar isn't happy.'

We could well understand his concern as the chanting increased: 'Enoch! Enoch.' Echoed by: 'Out! Out! Out!'

By sheer weight of numbers the audience was already encroaching onto the stage. A figure appeared, not Enoch, but the slim, elegantly suited young university registrar. He was greeted with ironic cheers and then respectful silence.

'The number of people in this hall exceeds those permitted by the fire regulations,' he announced. 'The meeting is therefore cancelled.'

There were wild cheers and counter cries: 'Shame!' 'Freedom of Speech!'

After some confusion Janet sidled up to me.

'We've got an alternative venue in town,' she said. 'We're not going to let them win.'

We drove to a lowly public house in town but by the time we arrived Mr Powell had already given his talk and was being hustled away. He did not want to talk to the press so we had to interview Janet who was glowing with excitement.

'What did he say!' we demanded.

'He gave us some fascinating insights into Keynesian economics.'

'But what about immigration? What did he say about that?'

'He didn't say anything about immigration. We're economics students. That's what we asked him to talk about, economics, not immigration and he was brilliant!'

'But didn't he mention immigration at all?'

'Not at all.'

We were now the ones who were frustrated. We had not wanted a river of blood but a gentle little punch-up would have been welcome.

27

Since Roman times soldiers had been garrisoned in York and it was still a command headquarters as well as being the home for a number of regiments. The Press and the army got on well together finding each other mutually beneficial; we gave them publicity and they provided us with stories. As a former National Serviceman I enjoyed my links with the army and it should not have been a surprise when I received an invitation which had a sting in its tale: would I like to join one of the Yorkshire regiments in Belfast for a few days? The sting was that 'The Troubles' were then at their height and bombs were going off and people were being killed. I swotted up on some very recent history. Protestants in British Northern Ireland had been trying to get rid of the resident Catholics in their midst fearing that they might be forced to join the Republican Catholic south. The army had gone in to protect the Catholics only to be attacked by the IRA — the Irish Republican Army. The bombing and killing had escalated with a steady increase of army casualties. In England there was a growing feeling that the mad Irish were fighting the Battle of the Boyne all over again and should be left to sort it out among themselves. But we are English, said the Protestants — you can't abandon us.

Head office thought it was a wonderful idea to have a reporter over there in the midst of it all but it was a little disturbing when they said they would have to fix up extra insurance for me. Even more worrying a few days later the IRA murdered two soldiers — ambushing them when they went out of barracks to meet their Irish girl friends. Tension was rising across the water and Meriel was far from happy.

Worries about being thrust into the front line in Northern Ireland were temporarily pushed to one side with an announcement from the cathedral. A press conference was being called to which the national newspapers were also being invited. Uncomfortably sitting alongside the great reporters of Fleet Street we waited for the great news: the Central Tower of the cathedral was in danger of falling down and it would take £2m to stabilise it. Appeals were being launched. Something was nagging at me. How was this discovered, someone asked.

'Cracks in the masonry,' said the Minster architect. 'We put glass 'tell-tales' across the cracks and they broke confirming movement.

Then we dug into the foundations and found they were virtually nonexistent. We disguised these excavations as archaeological work to avoid causing alarm but it is now confirmed — the whole tower is sinking.'

I was struck dumb. I had missed a scoop.

28

I said goodbye to Meriel at four o'clock in the morning. It was still dark outside and I felt like a soldier going off to war. Meriel was calmer about it than I was, quite brisk in fact.

'You'll be fine,' she said. 'Just don't do anything silly.'

As if I would. I drove to Leeds Bradford airport with a grey dawn breaking. I had never driven a car from darkness into light before and it was a sobering experience. With my vivid imagination at work I thought of the soldiers in the First World War waiting fearfully in the darkness for the sun to rise, knowing that for many of them it was going to be their last day on earth. My morbid thoughts faded as the daylight strengthened and the tiny propeller-driven aircraft growled its way up through the clouds.

'If you look to the left you will see Blackpool Tower,' said the pilot over the intercom. And there it was, the top section sticking up above the fluffy white clouds and looking dangerously close. Holiday makers were not going to get much of a view of the sea front today. We landed at Belfast and it was like entering a war zone with soldiers everywhere.

'You will be met,' Bill Holmes, the army PRO had told me. 'They will have your description.'

I wondered what that would be: thin, nervous young man with moustache perhaps. All very cloak and dagger and I felt lonely and vulnerable waiting in the reception area with armed soldiers and policemen all around watching me with growing suspicion. Then two men approached one brisk and erect wearing a smart hacking jacket and corduroy trousers and the other slightly scruffy in crumpled trousers and open neck shirt. Despite the civilian clothes their bearing screamed army.

'Major Wilson,' said the smart one who then nodded to his companion: 'This is Sergeant Harrison. Take the bag Harrison.'

'Yes sir,' came the reply. I was not impressed with their undercover disguise, even in a busy street the pair of them would have stood out. Our mode of transport however was more in keeping with clandestine operations — it was a shabby Ford Cortina and when I climbed in I noticed two Stirling machine guns protruding from under the front seats.

'Good flight?' inquired the major as we

drove off. He was sitting half turned in the front seat sometimes looking at me but more often staring out through the back window.

'Sorry about the car,' he said. 'We have a pool of old bangers and we keep changing the colour and the number plates otherwise Paddy gets to know them. Now then, what have they told you about the IRA?'

I was given a succinct history lesson about 'The Troubles' as we drove into Belfast. Everything looked relatively normal until we hit the road blocks where police and armed soldiers were searching cars. The major held his ID card low on his lap for inspection. With no outward reaction the guard said: 'We'll just look in the boot.'

'Be my guest,' said the major.

My edginess was growing. There was tension in the air. Obviously bad things had been happening around here. The regiment had taken over an old flour mill as its headquarters, a solidly built Victorian structure surrounded by a twelve foot wall. As we drove past these outer 'defences' the major pointed out where the wall had clearly been rebuilt with new bricks and mortar.

'Car bomb,' he said. 'Nobody hurt but it shook the old place to its foundations. Everything was covered in flour — it came raining out of the floor boards and the ceilings. Hell of a mess.'

This was going to be my home for the next few days.

The colonel briefed me on his 'patch'. A patrol was going out that afternoon — would I like to join it? Well yes — that was after all the purpose of my visit.

Watching a squad of ridiculously young-looking boys carefully loading live ammunition into their rifles in the weapon pits made me realise that this was real. Everyone clambered into an armoured car, the officer in the front seat alongside the driver, me directly behind him; the rest of the patrol sat in silent rows behind me. A steel shutter with two eye slits came down over the windscreen immediately plunging the inside of the vehicle into a darkened gloom. The officer adjusted his armoured vest and buttoned an armoured collar around his throat. I imagined how a medieval knight must have felt seeing a hostile world through a narrow slit in his helmet. We were waved through two sets of gates designed like the barbican on an old castle, one gate opened at a time so no-one could rush inside.

'Like to see some art work?' shouted the officer above the clatter of the engine. 'Paddy can be quite artistic.'

I nodded.

'Take you round one of the estates then.'

He gave directions to the driver but I failed to understand how we could see let alone appreciate any art work when locked up in this noisy rattling tin can. The armoured car eventually stopped.

'Out!' shouted the officer. The back doors were flung open and the men were gone. The officer followed at a more leisurely pace and I followed him. We were on some waste ground at the end of a row of terrace houses the brick gable end of which was covered in paintings, Irish flags, masked men brandishing guns, and slogans: 'Death to the Brits.'

I looked around nervously. Our soldiers had formed a circle around us, some against walls others crouched behind hedges.

'We'll just walk over slowly and have a look,' said the officer. 'Don't hurry.'

The officer leisurely pointed out some finer points of detail but I could not help noticing that people were coming out of their houses; this rather distracted my appreciation of the art work.

'Right,' said the officer. 'We'll wander back now. Don't want to stir up the natives too much.'

Someone somewhere started banging a dustbin lid. The officer made a signal and the soldiers retreated slowly back to their transport, unhurriedly he got back in himself and I joined him trying to look equally unconcerned. The rear doors of the armoured car clanged shut and we drove off but two sharp bangs nearly made me jump out of my skin.

'Just bricks,' said the officer. 'I'll take you to a more civilised part of town now.'

Eventually we 'debussed' in what looked like a normal shopping street but again the squaddies were out running ahead crouching in doorways and looking up at first floor windows.

'These are just reassurance visits,' explained our officer striding briskly along the pavement.

'How's it going?' he called to a shopkeeper standing in his doorway. 'All OK then?' The shopkeeper nodded and seemed more curious about me than the soldiers.

'You've got the press visiting you today,' said my escort chirpily. 'Seeing how you are getting on. Business as usual eh?'

Our cheery reassuring walk continued along the shopping street and ended at some broad crossroads. The officer stopped and pointed.

'Used to have problems here. Paddy put some snipers in those flats over there so this crossing got a bit hairy sometimes. We've sorted it out, so every now and then we have a little walk across here just to show them who's in charge — we are.'

He made no attempt to quicken his 'little walk' and I felt nervous sauntering beside him.

'We haven't lost a journalist yet,' he reassured me, 'and they'll know that's what you are by now. The jungle drums are very efficient round here.'

We returned to the relative safety of the shopping street and the armoured car but on the way back to the mill the driver got excited.

'That's him, sir, that's him,' I heard him telling the officer

The officer flung open the car door and in an instant he was out on the pavement. A man in a flat cap was standing smoking a cigarette on a street corner.

'You,' the officer shouted and the man was so startled the cigarette fell out of his mouth.

'Yes, you. We got the message. If anything happens we're coming after you, sunshine. We know where you live. We'll be coming after you.'

The man ran.

'Bastard,' muttered the officer as he got back into the car. 'That's put the fear of God into him.'

He saw the questioning look on my face

and hesitated. 'He was boasting in a pub the other night that they would get one of us before the week was out. The regiment was going to be targeted. Well now he's got something to think about.'

I looked at the silent faces of the men in the back of the armoured car and wondered what they were thinking. People out there were intent on murdering one of them before the week was out.

Once back in the flour mill the colonel was determined to keep me busy. I was whisked off to a barracks on the outskirts of the city. This was where the soldiers were stationed who were on extended tours of duty in Northern Ireland. The problem here, I was told, was women or rather the lack of them.

The colonel at the garrison barracks explained: 'You can't keep young lads locked up without female company for long periods of time — it's not natural but I'm not having any of my lads sneaking out and being murdered in honey traps so we've organized a few dances.'

I could hear the dance band warming up in the big drill hall but an officer took me down to the barrack gates. In the evening dusk a queue of girls stretched down the darkened street their warm top-coats half covering bright party frocks. The street lamps shone down on their heavily made-up faces. Two police women in uniform were searching handbags. The army was not averse to dancing with the 'enemy' as long as they had been frisked first. The dances were the highlight of the young soldiers' week and the squaddies added more information helped by plenty of nudges and winks.

'Know what I mean? Get the picture!'

I got the picture and the colonel obviously did too.

'I don't care what they do with the girls as long as they don't get shot while they're doing it,' he said.

Next morning I was out on patrol again but this time with two policemen. They were large, imposing men well able to look after themselves but nevertheless the army provided them with a squad of armed men.

'Pretend they're not there,' said one of the officers. 'You just walk along with us.'

Policemen were regularly being murdered in Northern Ireland but off we strolled as calmly as if we were on a leisurely wander down an English country lane. How could they do this every day?

'The object of the exercise,' said the larger of the two men looking down at me as we walked, 'is to show everyone around here that the civilian police are still in charge. We are not under military law.'

This was not very convincing when moving ahead of us on either side of the road were soldiers with their rifles cocked and behind us came more soldiers walking backwards, their heads constantly turning. The police officers must have sensed my doubts.

'We are still in charge,' repeated the officer. His companion added helpfully: 'Assisted by the army where necessary of course'.

There followed stories of ambushes and booby traps and my admiration for these men grew. Unlike the soldiers who every night retired behind high walls these men lived in the dangerous community they were protecting — everyone knew who they were and where they lived.

There was a rustle of activity ahead of us. The soldiers stopped and crouched in doorways and garden gateways. One of the police officers laid a hand on my arm and pulled me back.

'They're checking something,' he said, 'we'll just wait for a bit. I saw two soldiers running ahead of us up the street. One of the police officers lit a cigarette.

'Usually pretty quiet up here,' he said as a scruffy teenager walked past us furtively.

'Keeping out of bad company are yer, Michael?' said the police officer taking the cigarette out of his mouth. The youth muttered something and quickened his pace.

'You watch yourself now, do yer hear me?' the officer shouted after him.

'He's a wrong 'un is that,' said the other policeman.

But we were on the move again proudly walking up the middle of the street proving once again that the police were still in charge; I just wished they would not flaunt the fact when I was with them.

What was the reason for the delay? The NCO in charge, a self-confident young man from Leeds, explained: 'There was a bedroom window wide open, facing down the street, Not likely in this weather is it? Thought it could be a sniper. So we took a look-see but it was just a bloke painting his bedroom. Letting the paint smell out.'

I felt sorry for the DIY householder happily redecorating his bedroom and having two squaddies burst in on him with guns. The foot patrol with me in attendance passed through the housing estate without further incident but I was glad to be back behind the twelve foot walls of the old flour mill.

I interviewed a group of young soldiers and gathered their collective impressions. They had only been in the province a few weeks and it was all new and exciting, real soldiering, they said, out on the streets with a whiff of danger in the air. I wondered if they would still be as enthusiastic if the IRA kept their promise and 'got' one of them before the end of the week.

The visit ended and I was whisked back to the airport by my two-man under-cover team. We used another battered vehicle from what must have been the army's strangest motor pool. The small aircraft was filled with noisy, boisterous young men going home on leave. The solitary air hostess appeared to appreciative wolf howls and demonstrated how to fasten the lifejackets. She pirouetted to show the rear fastenings provoking more shouts and whistles.

One man in civilian clothes, clearly an officer, studiously read his newspaper and pretended not to hear. It was too dark to see Blackpool Tower on the return journey and the weather closed in. The plane started to shake and pitch as rain lashed the windows. A brilliant flash lit up the cabin and there was a clap of thunder. The plane bucked and shuddered. Through the rain-streaked windows I could see the lights of a large town as the plane descended, swaying and shaking — a heavy bump and we landed. The engines were switched off and there was just the beating of the rain on the windows.

A nervous silence was broken by a voice from the back of the plane: 'All right lads, let's hear it for the pilot.'

There was a desultory round of applause. I was safely home, I could walk down a street again without looking nervously over my shoulder; back there a war was raging.

29

I was back to a more mundane world with the central tower of the cathedral about to fall down. Ahead lay years of restoration work and the cathedral became a constant source of stories and hundreds of articles. Archaeologists worked ahead of the builders and engineers exploring and recording layers of history in the ground under the tower while impatiently at their elbows came the engineers waiting to pour concrete into the new foundations.

Sir Mortimer Wheeler, the famed archaeologist came, advised and held dramatic press conferences, moustache quivering, eyes sparkling with enthusiasm and despite his advancing years completely dazzling the lady reporters.

'My dear you come and sit by me,' he would say. 'I bet you have all sorts of fascinating questions you want to ask me. Yes?'

Most of them were too overawed to speak but it did not matter because Sir Mortimer was more into lecturing than question answering. To my delight the archaeologists did get down to the Romans, unearthing the stone drums that had made-up one of the pillars in the town's Roman forum nearly two thousand years before. And they were going to re-erect it outside the cathedral — another attraction for the tourist trade. Who said history was bunk?

It was a relief to get away from the cathedral and interview the Archbishop's chauffeur about the new car. His Grace's Victorian Gothic palace nestled among trees along the river bank on the outskirts of a small village; it exuded peace and calm. The archbishop's venerable Rolls Royce had been 'retired' and replaced with a Bentley which the chauffeur was polishing lovingly when George and I arrived. The car had a whole Victorian stable block and carriage store to itself and the chauffeur was enthusiastic about his new toy.

'It's got an automatic gearbox and power-assisted steering,' said the chauffeur proudly. This sounded very impressive indeed for someone whose basic Ford possessed no such marvels but in the write-up I got it wrong. The report read next day: 'The Archbishop of York's new car has a power assisted gearbox and automatic steering.'

I waited for retribution but there was none only a note from the news-desk to look out for a letter 'about your piece' that was going in the Letters Column the following day.

'Dear Sir (it said)

Reference your article about the Archbishop of York's new car. I can accept that God guides the Archbishop along the paths of righteousness when he is on foot but I cannot accept that He automatically steers His Grace's new Bentley.'

★   ★   ★

I was having twitchings of ambition again but with our new house and a daughter at school I could work up no real enthusiasm for actually moving. Life was comfortable. Perhaps I could overcome this feeling of divine discontent without actually moving at all. I had an idea. Romans lurked everywhere under the city and I had become more and more fascinated with them. When footings were dug for new buildings, there were the reminders of the Romans with their barrack blocks and bath houses. They intrigued me so much so that I decided to write a book. I would become a famous author and escape from the daily chore of news-gathering, With a portable typewriter on the kitchen table I sought my escape and typed late into the night. I marched at the head of my legions and conquered Yorkshire and as I conquered I dreamed dreams. When the film rights were sold, I told myself, it would be in the contract that I could be an extra in the battle scenes. The news-camera men visiting the set would be told: 'The author chap is over there in the third cohort from the left.' And I would give a modest, unassuming interview before launching myself at the Brigantes, the local war-like tribe, and dying heroically on camera.

They were wonderful dreams but I felt vulnerable and apprehensive as I wrapped the book into a parcel and posted it off to Longmans. I was letting someone else into my dream and I feared they were going to smash it to pieces. The precious parcel was handed over the counter at the village post office and a few days later a national postal strike brought all mail in the country to a standstill.

30

I sank back into my real world and became an expert on collapsing cathedrals. Weekly press conferences were held to explain what was going on, stabilising the old foundations of the tower by wrapping them round with concrete and securing everything with huge steel bolts.

Tucked away behind the cathedral was the stonemasons' yard another world within the city to which I now became a regular visitor. It was a world where time had slowed as the masons and stone carvers worked silently at their benches. The entrance to the yard was dominated by a stone cutting saw, an awe-inspiring device with a long blade suspended between two swinging arms slowly cutting its way through gigantic pieces of limestone onto which water was constantly spraying. The blade swung to and fro cutting the stone at a steady six inches an hour its slow steady pace somehow symbolising the calm, steady heart beat of the place. What was the hurry? The cathedral had been there for hundreds of years and it would be there for hundreds more if not for eternity.

I was constantly in the cathedral climbing up into the rafters, scaling vertical iron ladders to inspect crumbling pinnacles, watching the stained glass being repaired and gargoyles being shaped; something was always happening in the Minster.

★ ★ ★

And then: 'Dad, why can't we go with you?'

George and I were going up into the Dales to cover an agricultural show and the stars of a popular television vet series were going to put in an appearance.

'Because I'm going in George's car — we always go in George's car.'

'But why couldn't he take us as well? We'd be no bother — honest.'

'We' in this case were Penny and her friend Joanna. Meriel entered the fray.

'For goodness sake why not? Ask George to take them as well — he won't bite.'

'There's the damn dog,' I said. 'He might.'

'Joanna loves dogs,' said Penny so that excuse was overridden.

To my surprise George the dragon did not mind at all and he even called at our house to pick everyone up. The girls both in their teens were dressed for a day out. Penny having heard numerous tales of George's flashes of

140

temper must have passed the information on to Joanna. She soon had the Yorkshire terrier down from its shelf behind the back seat and was re-arranging the bow on the top of its head. I could not understand how George, the most masculine of men, could put a pretty blue bow on his dog's head. Silence reigned in the car as we headed for the hills — the girls were either playing with the dog or whispering among themselves. George was impressed. I suspected he was not used to the social graces that young girls can display when so minded in contrast perhaps to his two very normal teenage sons.

The sun shone and it was a glorious day. The television stars of All Creatures Great and Small paraded around the show-ring in a farm cart pulled by a tractor and then went walk-about. We gave the girls a meeting point and everyone went about their business. When we met up with them later for lunch in one of the marquees they were in a high state of excitement. Back in the car they still had their heads together whispering.

'What's the matter with you two?' I demanded.

'Nothing,' said Penny.

'Nothing,' said Joanna.

There clearly was but they were not telling. On the way home George stopped the car in a small market town.

'Wait one,' he said in brisk military mode. He went into a little souvenir shop and returned with four huge ice-cream cornets. This was a George I had not seen before.

From the girls came a polite chorus of: 'Thank you Mr Stott.' We sat in the town square licking our ice-creams with the sun beating down on us. There was still more whispering in the back seat which I decided to ignore.

'Can we give the dog what's left of the cornets please?'

The terrier perched on the back shelf had been going quietly berserk, its head flicking hungrily side to side watching the slowly vanishing cornets. George had ordered it to sit and sit it did, paws obediently glued to the back shelf but all the other sinews in its tiny body were twitching in anticipation. Permission granted, Joanna collected the remains of the cornets and they vanished inside the Yorkshire terrier with the swift efficiency of a vacuum cleaner. A splattering of ice-cream on the dog's fur was removed with Joanna's handkerchief. She really did like dogs. But then they were back to whispering.

'Now come on,' I said. 'What's up with you two?'

The two girls exchanged glances.

'Come on' I demanded.

Joanna with a wave of the hand indicated that Penny should be spokesperson.

'He winked at us,' said Penny.

'Who did?'

'You know! He did,' and she named the young, good looking star of the show.

'And he smiled,' said Joanna. 'He winked at us and he smiled — at us.

'Wow,' I said.

'Yes dad, wow!' said Penny crossly and I realised almost too late that I was in serious danger of spoiling a magic moment. I retreated rapidly.

'Probably winks at all the pretty girls,' I said.

'Wait till I tell them at school,' said Joanna.

'He's really good looking,' said Penny.

It had been a normal day's work for George and I but a memorable one for the girls. God bless you Christopher Timothy — you smiled and winked at my daughter and quite made her day.

31

Another triennial festival was upon us. It was disturbing how quickly these three-year events came around and how the same stories surfaced but with different names. David Bradley, an actor little known at the time, was to play Christ in the medieval Mystery Plays. Much later in life he would appear as Filch, the caretaker of Hogwarts School in the Harry Potter films. Two bit part players in the production reported after the first rehearsal that he was 'really nice.'

Penny and Joanna were in the vast cast and enthusiastically attended rehearsals and afterwards regaled us with all the gossip. We could not keep track of the different roles they were playing. Every time we asked they were doing something different. Much later we learned why there had been so much role changing. Their first job had been looking after the sheep in a pastoral scene but they left the pen open and the animals escaped and ran about under the stage causing mayhem. Then they were among the weeping women under the cross but on the first night they had a fit of giggles. With a forgiving Christian attitude that was almost saint-like the director decided that there were too many spectators at the crucifixion; the girls were given other roles. Penny had a 'baby' torn from her arms and 'killed' during The Murder of the Innocents and then appeared demurely as an angel in Heaven. She and Joanna cheered and waved their palm branches as Christ entered Jerusalem and then got speaking roles. 'Crucify Him,' they yelled in the trial scenes. They had the time of their lives and never forgot David Bradley.

★　★　★

The explosion shook the house. Meriel reached for the bedside light and knocked the supper cups crashing onto the floor. Mother and father were staying with us and I heard father shouting from the bedroom next door: 'Don't worry! It's just the lifeboat.'

As we were some forty miles from the sea this was unlikely. My parents lived on the coast and in his half-conscious state at three in the morning father thought he was still at home and someone had let off a maroon to call out the lifeboat crews.

From the front room window I could see the orange glow of fires and black smoke coming from the army camp on the outskirts of the village. Napoleon once said: 'If in doubt march towards the sound of the guns.' It seemed good advice so I drove in the direction of the flames.

Behind the army security fence one of the wooden barrack blocks was blazing. I abandoned the car and walked across the open moor to get a closer look. A loud crackling noise like a spluttering machine gun was coming from the asbestos sheets of the roof. I stood helplessly outside the fence as the building burned. There were no fire engines, no police, nothing, but then I became aware of a figure walking along on the other side of the fence.

'Is anyone hurt?' I shouted to him. He came closer and I saw it was a man wearing an army overcoat over his pyjamas.

'No-one's hurt,' he said and we both stood on either side of the fence staring as the flames and sparks leapt higher.

'What on earth happened?'

'Suspiciously like a bomb,' said the man in a very cultured calm voice. 'By the way, who the Hell are you if I may ask?'

I explained who I was as a distant wailing announced the approach of police cars and fire engines.

'Thank goodness the hut was empty,' I said.

'It wasn't actually empty,' said the man. 'All the regiment's band instruments were in there.'

Firemen now appeared inside the camp and more soldiers. A police siren wailed behind me and I saw a police car with lights flashing racing towards me down the track over the moor.

'I'll leave you to it then,' said my companion. 'But you'd better have a word with those chaps first.'

Two figures in uniform were running towards me. It occurred to me that they could be armed so I remained stock-still; fortunately the leading policeman recognised me and I him.

'Oh it's you,' he said and there was bitter disappointment in his voice. 'What are you doing here?'

'I live just down the road.'

Stern fingers were wagged at me. 'We'll want to talk to you.'

More police arrived and I convinced them that I had seen nothing on my dash to the scene. I was allowed to go back home where the family was having an early breakfast. Urgent phone calls aroused head office staff to get out an early edition of the evening paper.

'THE DAY THEY BOMBED THE

BAND' shouted the headlines.

The intruders had cut through the perimeter wire and in the darkness planted explosives under the nearest block of wooden barrack rooms. If they had been filled with sleeping soldiers they would have been incinerated as they slept. The cold blooded callousness of it chilled everyone. And this had happened just outside our village. These people had probably wandered down our front street. 'The Troubles' were spreading into our backyard.

A few weeks later there were more bombs and this time, deaths: an army minibus was blown up on the M62. Intelligence reports said it was the work of the same IRA 'team' that had visited our village. Everyone was nervous. There was a 'team' wandering around our peaceful corner of England trying to kill people and they were succeeding.

32

'I've had a phone call and you'll never guess who it was. Go on have a guess.'

This always infuriated me.

'Just tell me,' I demanded.

'Go on guess!' said Meriel.

'Tell me!'

'Longmans! They're going to publish your book. You've got to go to London and talk to them about it.'

Incredible! I was going to be an author. No more worrying over news lists! No more daily deadlines! I spoke to a Mr Guest at Longman's on the telephone. Yes, they were going to publish my book but would I care to 'pop up to town' next week to discuss the details. Yes, I most certainly could.

The new author-to-be took the breakfast train to Kings Cross but without partaking of the breakfast being served in the restaurant car; perhaps next time he could afford to travel First Class. He did however feel the occasion warranted a taxi to his publishers. Longman's premises were dark and Dickensian and Mr Guest was charmingly complimentary about my book. But instead of getting down to details I was taken on a trip around the office to meet other members of the staff.

'His book has a lovely Roman feel to it,' said Mr Guest and I felt very important indeed but wondered when we were going to get down to business? My publisher-to-be however was studying his watch.

'There is one important matter we have to settle but we can discuss that over lunch.'

I was led out of the building and down the street to a very smart steakhouse where the prices on the menu were ridiculous.

'I'm going to have a minute steak with salad,' said Mr Guest helpfully.

'And I will have the same,' I said.

'Now to business: The title of your book . . . I don't like it at all. It won't do.'

He looked at me guardedly as if expecting noisy protests. I could not care less what they called it!

'The definite article,' he suddenly announced.

What on earth was the man talking about?

'So important in a book title — The! It's strong! Eye catching! Don't you agree?'

Of course I agreed if he thought so.

'The General. The Gun. Marvellous titles! So we will call your book . . . '

And there was a dramatic pause.

'The Provincial Governor!'

I was not overwhelmed.

'You agree?'

'That will be fine,' I said as the steaks and salad arrived.

'Jolly, jolly good. Now we can enjoy our lunch.'

That was it? I had paid out good money on a rail ticket and the luxury of a taxi to come all this way just to agree to a name change? My Yorkshire hackles rose. What a waste of money! I regretted not ordering a larger steak.

'We'll sort out a couple of other matters in the office,' said Mr Guest before chatting at length about the publishing trade. He called for the bill which arrived on a silver salver. I expected a display of crisp ten pound notes as he opened his wallet but instead he produced a thick wodge of luncheon vouchers and began carefully to count them out onto the salver. He pinned them down with a handful of coins.

We returned to the office and my manuscript was taken out of a drawer and put on the desk. It looked crumpled as if it had passed through many hands.

'I think you wrote this rather hurriedly,' said Mr Guest hesitantly. I nodded.

'And without the benefit of a proof reader I suspect,' again the hesitation and again my acquiescence.

'I would like you to go through it all again very carefully. Your punctuation . . . spelling . . . ? Not quite ready to go to the printers I think. So could I ask you . . . ?'

The battered manuscript was pushed gently towards me. It was coming back to me again. This was not what I had expected.

'But you are going to publish it?' I demanded.

'Most certainly, an excellent novel. Good solid book for the libraries. It just needs a little tidying up and perhaps a little tweak at the end. Last words are so important. Have a look at it. See what you think. I'll get one of the girls to wrap it up for you.'

I walked out into the busy London streets with my great unpublished novel under my arm and slowly started to feel important again. I deserved a treat so I went into Lyons Corner House for tea and a cake. I uneasily recalled the first time that I had encountered the Corner House waitresses in their black uniforms and white caps. Then they had been a huddled group of middle-aged ladies nervously wondering how to cope with myself and a gang of other soldiers all belligerently shouting: 'Don't close the Stage Door Canteen!'

On National Service I had been stationed in London and we had access to the Stage

Door Canteen in an old building off Piccadilly — it was our second home with free variety shows every night and cheap food. But it was owned by Lyons Corner House and they wanted it back. Somehow I found myself carried along in a protest demonstration. We had poured into the Victorian splendour of the tea-room in Piccadilly and the usual customers fled as we took over the tables chanting our battle cries.

'Oh come on dearies,' pleaded the waitresses. 'We don't want any trouble do we, now please — be good boys.'

The chanting and shouting eventually died away and we found ourselves marooned in one corner of the vast tea-room, starkly empty but for us and a huddle of whispering waitresses. As a protest group we lacked authority and numbers and an embarrassing silence descended. Then the doors opened and a dozen military police marched in. They were big terrifying men with their peaked caps down over their eyes and a collective shiver went through us protesters. One of the policemen, a sergeant, strode forward and looked at us for a very long time. I seriously wondered if at a given signal his men would pounce and we would be beaten to a pulp and our corpses charged with mutiny — military police induced that sort of fear in little National Servicemen.

'You will all stand up very quietly,' said the sergeant. 'Then you will put your chairs back neatly under the tables, and you will all walk slowly out through that door. And you will not, I repeat not, come back here again. Do I make myself clear?'

There were dumb nods.

'Right! Everyone — out!'

Like the good little boys we were we departed, and not long after they did close the Stage Door Canteen and it became a restaurant again. The war, after all, was over. I looked around Lyons Corner House again and remembered fonder memories. Meriel and I came here on our honeymoon. This time however I was alone and I sipped my tea and made my cake last as long as possible by breaking it into tiny morsels with the dainty little cake fork. I stared at the brown paper parcel beside me. Was this the turning point — the beginning of my new life?

I was still day-dreaming as I walked out into Piccadilly. Someone bumped into me heavily, muttered an apology, and was gone. It was several minutes before I realised my wallet had gone too. I was stunned, standing in Piccadilly with the world going by all around me, busy and uncaring, miles from home with no rail ticket and no money to buy another. My cosy day-dreaming ended abruptly. What to do? Go back to Longmans and ask for an advance on royalties? Too humiliating. I told myself that in a crisis one should ask a policeman.

'You're in luck sir,' said the very tall officer looking down at me and oozing unhurried calm. 'There's a police station just down there. They'll look after you.'

And they did but with a hint of weariness that left me feeling like a gormless country mouse lost in the big city. A brisk young detective took down the details and gave me a detailed account of the skills of London pickpockets. He clearly admired their expertise.

'Your wallet will turn up,' he said. 'They're only after the cash — they'll dump the rest. Lyons Corner House was it? Probably dump it in a lavatory cistern — that's what they usually do.'

Just an everyday occurrence then. Nothing to get excited about. With only a few coins in my trouser pocket I walked a long way back to King's Cross Station. The police had not inquired how I was going to get home — that was my problem. At King's Cross I asked a porter the way to the Stationmaster's Office. Gerald Nabarro, MP was right — journalism did give young men a cheeky amount of confidence.

'I'm afraid I'm in trouble,' I told the stationmaster. 'Someone has stolen my wallet and my return ticket was in it. I've got a police crime report.'

I put the document on his desk as proof. 'My dad was the stationmaster at Scarborough,' I said. 'I remember him telling me it is possible to help people out when this sort of thing happens.'

Sitting behind his large desk in a room that looked like a Victorian parlour the stationmaster was awesomely impressive. I began to feel nervous about my boldness.

'You must be Bill Scott's son then.'

Thank heavens for railwaymen! Even though the good old London and Northern Eastern Railway Company had disappeared into British Rail the company camaraderie was still there — the stationmaster knew my dad and I was given a warrant to get me home.

A week later I received a parcel. It was my wallet with all my papers still in it but no cash. It had been found, as the detective prophesised, stuffed into a lavatory cistern in Lyon's Corner House. The police had kindly dried out the contents before sending it on. I sent the unused return ticket to the friendly stationmaster at King's Cross with a thank-you letter and got down to proof reading my manuscript; I felt ashamed at the misspellings but then my arrogant defence mechanism cut in — didn't Longmans have sub-editors? Surely it was their job to sort out such trivial matters as the odd comma and full stop.

33

With fame and authorship looming I reflected on the world I felt I would soon be leaving. What was our role? We scurried around as professional observers poking our noses into everyone's business, sometimes wanted sometimes not. We moved freely in and out of other people's lives adapting like chameleons to whatever company we were in — sometimes an angry lord complaining about walkers on his grouse moors and then the mum in her council house surveying the remains of her kitchen after a chip-pan fire. We went everywhere and talked to everyone. It never occurred to me that we, mere observers, might also be important — that was left to the national reporters who occasionally visited us. It was the industrial correspondents, the supposed experts on the activities of the all powerful trade unions, who thought themselves important. An organisation called the Confederation of Shipbuilding and Engineering Unions held regular meetings in our town. Stout, solid union leaders in their best suits gathered once a month in the station hotel and discussed pay deals and inter-union disputes in smoke-filled rooms. The industrial correspondents hovered around them like moths around a flame occupying the armchairs and sofas in the hotel lounge and ordering endless trays of coffee and biscuits on expenses while union matters were discussed in secret behind closed doors.

We, the local reporters, hung around the fringes trying to glean what was going in this mysterious secretive world waiting for hours for a door to open and for someone to give us a statement.

'Nowt much for you lads this month,' was the usual greeting from the big man behind the table with his ash tray full of cigarette stubs as a proud testament to the efforts of the day.

'What about the pay demand?' asked the Times.

'Employers still considering it.'

'And the welders' dispute?' asked the Express.

'More talks next week.'

'You must have been discussing something,' said the Daily Telegraph with exasperation in his voice.

The chairman shuffled his papers and thought for a while.

'Well yes, we have been discussing world peace.'

We waited for some revelation but nothing more was forthcoming.

'Can we assume you are in favour of it?' asked the Telegraph.

It was such moments that made the waiting worthwhile.

★ ★ ★

Regularly we received long letters from mother with news from Wales. Elderly relatives all sent their love. Aunt Nell died but we did not go to the funeral. Our excuse was that we did not want to take Penny from school. And then Auntie Katie 'slipped away'. That was the phrase mother used and it seemed so appropriate for that gentle soul. I remembered her standing on the corner outside the bread shop, ghost-like, waving us goodbye. I remembered her with tears in her eyes when she first saw Penny; it was far too easy to imagine her thoughts. To me her life seemed such a sad waste. All the characters from my childhood were slipping away leaving just memories.

Uncle Bob the Baker was taken into a home but mother would have none of it and she brought him out and she and father looked after him. Soon there was another letter from mother: 'I don't think he is going to be with us long. I know you loved your Uncle Bob so I thought you might want to come and see him.' The words that should have followed were not on the page but I knew what they would have been: 'before he dies'.

I pictured that burly flour-speckled figure, king of the bake-house, with those scalding hot tins of crackling fresh bread cascading out of the searing-hot ovens. I found a shrunken figure propped up by pillows in an armchair. And a few weeks later I made the journey again for his funeral and helped Ivor and Ellis his nephews carry his coffin into and out of the chapel. With that weight on my shoulder and all my childhood memories churning I thought perhaps that this was it at last, catharsis, the end of all that mournful Welsh nostalgia. But of course it wasn't.

<h1 style="text-align:center">34</h1>

There were whispers of a corruption inquiry into the council. This sounded exciting but nothing could be confirmed until an announcement was made that Scotland Yard had been called in to investigate. Suddenly the gossip was buzzing. A superintendent and a sergeant arrived from London and worked in secrecy which only added to the rumour mill. What was going on? I received a phone call. The Scotland Yard superintendent wanted to interview me. The great man sat behind his desk, arms folded, not saying a word while the sergeant paced up and down doing all the talking.

'You've been reporting on the council now for a good few years I believe. You must know what goes on there.'

'I would say so,' I said.

'Senior journalist,' he said. 'People must confide in you, tell you things.'

Flattery, I knew, but yes, there had been our informant on Lord Esher's plans.

'It has happened,' I acknowledged.

'So has anyone talked to you recently?'

'About what?'

Sergeant and superintendent exchanged glances.

'Back-handers, dodgy contracts,' said the sergeant.

'Not a whisper,' I said.

'Heard any names mentioned?'

'Not a word,' I said. 'In fact I'd be astonished if anything like that was going on with this council.'

The superintendent raised his head and for the first time looked interested.

'Why do you say that?' he demanded.

'Because I don't think the political situation here gives anyone much chance for fiddling,' I said. 'We've got two political parties evenly balanced and they watch each other like hawks. I doubt if they could get away with anything dodgy. Anyway no group's in power long enough.'

'Very interesting,' said the superintendent. 'So as someone with his ear to the ground you've heard nothing.'

'Nothing,' I said. 'In fact we're all very surprised you're here. Is there anything you can tell me?' I asked. 'What is this all about?

'Early days,' said the sergeant briskly. 'But thank you. You've been very helpful.'

'Perhaps you could let me know if . . . '

'We'll be making a statement, eventually.'

I left feeling disturbed and then angry

when I realised why. Would a Fleet Street journalist have been so gushingly forthcoming? Should I not have said to Scotland Yard: 'Yes I know a great deal about the workings of this council but what can you tell me first?'

'What did they want?' everyone demanded in the office.

'They wanted to know if I knew anything dodgy about the council,' I said, 'which I didn't.'

A telephone call broke up my feelings of failure.

'Hi,' said Bill the army public relations officer, 'You've been to Ireland — fancy joining a Yorkshire regiment on a NATO exercise in Germany? Out in the field with the lads, just the job for a fit young chap like you.'

'You're on.' I said.

We learned later that a highly respected alderman had been the subject of the inquiry having been wrongly accused of malpractice in a series of anonymous poison-pen letters. The writer was discovered to be a young disgruntled businessman who ended up in court himself. Our council was not a hotbed of corruption after all. At least my assessment of our local politicians had been correct.

★ ★ ★

Normality returned and its routines. Monday night was theatre night with a pool of repertory actors and actresses performing a different play every week. For Meriel and I it was like joining a weekly family gathering and having the best seats in the house. We sat on one side of the aisle and the critic from the local paper sat on the other with his wife. Around us was a scattering of elderly couples, all familiar faces, occupying the same seats week after week as regularly as church goers.

When the curtain went up there would be a ripple of polite applause for the set designer and then when a favourite performer made their first appearance, usually someone ancient to our young eyes, there would be welcoming applause. The actor (or actress) would give a gracious nod of acknowledgement before he or she slipped into the role they were playing that particular week. We were all part of a happy community sharing and enjoying a make-believe world newly created every week for our entertainment.

Talented young things did appear from time to time to sparkle and dazzle in our provincial backwater but the brighter they sparkled the quicker they disappeared. We saw their names in West End reviews, sometimes even on the screen in the local cinema and then we proudly told friends: 'I saw him/her when they were at the theatre'.

The newspaper's review deadline was 9.30pm which meant telephoning from the public phone in the foyer during the second interval. I lived in fear that an actor really would drop down dead during the third act of an Agatha Christie thriller while a benign review praising his performance appeared in the paper the next day.

Daughter Penny took over as my companion and advisor during the panto season when comic animals cavorted through the audience distributing sweets. The animals paid her a great deal of attention — the theatre director was no fool.

As part of our small cosy world at Christmas a box of chocolates would arrive from the local confectionary factory and there were other gifts. Mrs Locke, the advertisement lady in the front office, dreaded the 'glorious twelve', the day when mass murder was done on the grouse moors. A burly gamekeeper wearing knickerbockers and gaiters would stomp heavy-booted into the front office and dump a brace of birds on her nicely-polished counter.

They were an aristocratic form of payment in kind for George who was a well-known figure at all the county weddings, hunt balls, game fairs and the shoots.

★　★　★

The design cover for my book arrived, a lurid fiery red affair slashed across with the standard of a Roman legion.

'I hope you're not expecting too much out of this,' said Meriel.

'We'll have to make some work decisions after the next book is published,' I said confidently.

'The next one?'

Meriel's tone was incredulous but a telephone call from Leeds broke off the discussion. Would I like a job at head office as a sub-editor? Sub-editors were considered a step above reporters although reporters were loath to concede that. I brooded. It would mean working in Leeds at night, commuting every day, trapped inside an office, never getting out to meet people, never being there when things were happening. I would also be juggling with other people's words not my own and I had a daughter growing up. I would only see her fleetingly before setting off to work every evening. I might even have to move but this was an offer of promotion, someone at Head Office thought I was capable of better things? I brooded and finally decided: 'No thank you,' I said and afterwards I lay awake at night wondering if I had done the right thing. But did it really matter — was I not going to become an author?

35

I was trying to sleep in my smelly sleeping bag inside a tiny tent on a school car park in Germany. The bag reeked of some kind of greasy disinfectant which probably kept the bugs at bay but did nothing for the hardness of the tarmac. All around me soldiers were curled up and fast asleep in their vehicles. We were part of Blue Force hiding under camouflage and getting some rest before facing the invading Reds. At first light the lieutenant stuck his head through the tent flap and I was invited to join him and the rest of the company for 'ablutions'. These were in a school which had been taken over by the army for the duration of the 'war'. It was an infants' school with low, tiny washbasins now dwarfed by burly soldiery washing and shaving. After hardly any sleep and aching from my tarmac mattress I faced the prospect of my first day of battle.

'Let's see if we can find you some action,' said the lieutenant getting out his map. 'B company are supposed to be in a wood not far from here. They should have dug themselves in and 'cammed-up.'' This was army-speak for hiding.

We found the wood, parked the jeep and continued on foot. A figure with a rifle rose from the shrubs at the edge of the trees and shouted: 'Who goes there?'

'It's me you dozy pratt,' said the officer.

The young soldier was taken aback.

'I need the password, sir.'

'Geronimo.'

The solder was confused.

'That was the password yesterday, sir. It's been changed.'

'So what the Hell is it today then?'

'It's Cromwell sir.'

'You daft bugger!' said the officer but now they were both laughing.

'B company's dug in about twenty yards further in, sir,' said the guard. And there they were concealed in trenches their faces daubed with camouflage paint. Bivouacs were covered with branches and machine-guns lay hidden behind fallen trees. We were directed though the defences to company headquarters — a mound of camouflage netting covering a tent. 'What exactly are you doing here?' I asked the company commander for it was obvious that nothing was happening.

'Hiding,' he said. 'We were given four hours to vanish before aerial reconnaissance tries to find us. We don't think the Reds know we're here yet but there's dew on that field so don't go walking across it — it leaves tracks. And if you hear a plane coming get out of sight damn quick.'

I got the impression that I could ruin the whole war with some careless footprints. For the soldiers patiently waiting to be attacked however a visit from the press relieved the boredom. They had been occupying the wood unmolested for two days and they wanted someone to attack them; they wanted to get 'stuck in', they wanted to mow down the red hordes with noisy blasts of blank ammunition. We visited other dug-in units and eventually found the senior officers concealed much more comfortably in an old barn; it was here that the the wider picture was revealed.

Blue army was dispersed at strategic geographical 'squeeze points' and waiting for the Reds to come; their role was to delay the advance for as long as possible. We passed a section of the autobahn that had been sealed off and was parked up with RAF jump-jets. The long straight autobahns, we were told, would become aircraft runways if . . .

When all the journalists were back in barracks we were given a briefing on the course of the 'war' and the stark realities of what the real thing could be like were spelled out for us. If the Cold War were to become hot then Russian tanks were expected to reach the English Channel in six weeks if opposed by non-nuclear weapons. Some conventional fighting however was considered necessary to create time for last minute peace attempts to be made. If these failed the war would then go nuclear. Areas along the Russian line of advance had already been identified and ear-marked for nuclear incineration. Armageddon in Europe would arrive in the shape of ten-inch nuclear shells fired from huge field howitzers. It was disturbing to think that this exercise was practising for what could be the end of the world.

To cheer us up that evening the journalists were split into groups and taken on a pub crawl. It was a garrison town and the beer halls were numerous and the entertainment astonishing. Films were being projected continuously onto the walls of one drinking den showing pornography of the most startling and imaginative kind, some of it in cartoon form. It was totally ignored by the solid beer-supping German regulars but not by the visiting squaddies and journalists. The atmosphere was starkly different from any English country pub. I tried not to watch what was happening on the walls but it was difficult to hold conversations because all English eyes were focussed in one direction.

If Walt Disney had known what Snow White, the prince and the seven dwarves really got up to he would have been put off fairy tales for life.

Next morning we were back in the front line watching from a windy hill-top as the infantry enthusiastically charged into a village at bayonet point. The cooks arrived with large tin boxes carrying our lunch. There were no tables, no chairs, this was Spartan in-the-field stuff eating standing up as the colonel explained the battle scene below us.

Braced against a near-gale-force wind we each received a paper plate and the cooks filed past us depositing first a slice of bread onto the plate, then a slice of ham, followed by a lettuce leaf topped up with a tomato — a DIY salad sandwich. I decided to eat my lunch piecemeal, which I discovered was a strategic error. I sank my teeth into the tomato. Freed from its stabilising weight the lettuce leaf began to tremble in the wind — suddenly it took off and fluttered across the field. The ham quivered and went off in pursuit. I made an ineffectual grab at the remaining piece of bread but was too late — that too went airborne. I was left clutching a paper plate and with a dripping tomato clenched between my teeth.

'Oh bad luck, Scott,' said the colonel as he

continued his briefing. I was reminded of Wellington at Waterloo when an officer beside him was wounded and cried out:

'By gad sir I've lost my leg!'

To which Wellington replied: 'By gad sir, so you have.'

What was a lost sandwich in comparison?

I made up for the loss by eating heartily in the barracks dining room that night. A few hours later I met a fellow journalist in the ablution block and we vied with each other for who could be the most dramatically sick. I think I won. We both agreed that unless Red Force was using chemical warfare we should not have chosen the chicken. And to make matters worse next day we were flying back home. We reported sick but got scant sympathy in the Medical Officer's surgery despite our civilian status. There had been a big party in the barracks the previous night and the doctor had had his fill of morning hang-overs. We did not even get to see him. We told his sergeant about our pitiful state and what chaos and embarrassment there could be on the plane if we travelled in our present condition. Our symptoms and fears were conveyed to a presence in the next room. After some muttering the sergeant returned with pills in two paper cups.

'They'll dry you up and get you home,' he

said. 'Don't drink so much next time.'

Don't drink so much! I hadn't touched a drop but what was the point in arguing?

I did get home but I never discovered what happened to my fellow sufferer. Perhaps he died and was buried en route because I was in bed for two days with violent stomach pains. I was put on a drug for easing child-birth pangs and I floated away on fluffy white clouds. My doctor said I was suffering from food poisoning made worse by the 'get-you-home pills.' They had certainly got me home but at the expense of dangerously trapping the food poison inside me. In my few lucid moments I wondered how much worse it might have been if I had caught and eaten that last flying piece of ham.

36

My book was published! It was up there on a shelf in W H Smiths. Every lunch hour I went to stare at it hoping in vain to see a queue of eager buyers. Another copy appeared in the Public Library and whenever I visited I checked how many times it had been taken out. I waited but no-one telephoned to discuss the film rights. My Walter Mitty dream faded. The mountain had given forth a mouse. It did not make it any easier that a dreaded 'slow news-day' was upon us. We were searching the courts for a story, any story, with the four o'clock deadline approaching and the news 'bucket' nearly empty.

The clanging of a distant fire engine raised hopes. There was an 'incident' not a fire, near the medieval King's Manor where an archaeological dig was in progress. I knew about this dig — they were trying to find an old tower buried underneath the ramparts of the medieval wall which still surrounded the city. Traces of it had been found in Victorian times but it had never been fully explored so archaeologists were digging into the ramparts to try and find it again. I wandered down to see what was happening and found a strangely silent watching crowd. The tunnel into the earth embankment had collapsed and one of the archaeologists was buried. I saw his colleagues watching, ashen-faced as the firemen dug into the fresh soil. Whispered questions revealed the name. I knew him well, he had often enthusiastically explained to me the significance of some unpromising piece of masonry he had uncovered deep in the ground. The silent arrival of an ambulance grimly suggested that a bell-ringing display of urgency was no longer necessary. He would not be found alive.

I had always been emotionally detached when reporting deaths but this was someone I knew. The death cast a shadow over the tightly knit world of archaeologists in the city. Some years later they did find the tower and it was opened up for display with a little plaque commemorating the tragedy.

*　*　*

Despite the silence that greeted my book I started writing another. The last book had been about a heroic Roman commander. The next one would be about a cowardly Roman swept along by the tide of great events. At least it would be different. My reasoning was

that in this world there were far more cowardly losers than heroic winners; I reasoned
therefore that there were more people likely to
identify themselves with my fictional 'non-
hero'. How wrong could one be?

Another call from Leeds — could I do a
fortnight's holiday relief at our London
Office? Why did people insist on disturbing
me in my comfortable rut? So now I was
working in Fleet Street in an office which had
not changed much since Charles Dickens
popped out of the House of Commons to do
a quick Parliamentary sketch. Although
London Office sounded important it con-
sisted, editorially, of one charming, patrician
figure whose by-line appeared regularly in the
newspaper, and myself.

'Soon get the hang of the geography,' he
said.

I explained that I had walked these streets
before as a soldier doing National Service in
the War Office in Whitehall and he looked
mildly impressed. So I manned the London
News Desk of the Yorkshire Post on a regular
evening shift while he worked elsewhere in
the building writing 'think pieces' about the
great issues of the day. I waited by the telephone terrified in case Head Office demanded
a quick quote from the Prime Minster or
worse from Buckingham Palace. Occasionally

the London Editor would interrupt my careful hunt through The Times for Yorkshire obituaries and present me with a sheaf of paper fresh from the machine in the next room which was constantly chattering out agency reports.

'Change the intro a bit,' he said. 'Cut it by half and send it through. Mark it 'From our London Staff'.'

It duly appeared on the front page the next day. I kept a lonely vigil on the night news desk never once having to use the contact book with the names and telephone numbers of Government spokesmen and other 'reliable sources'.

I was singularly unimpressed with the Street of Ink, but again this was a district office, there were no great beasts of printing presses lurking below to thunder out copies of one's words and rush them out into the streets. It was all so painfully quiet.

One night I was given tickets to review a West End play, Hedda Gabler by Ibsen. I enjoyed doing theatre reviews even though at home I sometimes upset the local amateurs with my criticisms; my view was that if people paid good money for a seat they were entitled to good entertainment, not an egotistical display by a mutual admiration society. Not surprisingly therefore I was impressed by the professionalism of the West End show and said so. The London Editor wandered in with my theatre copy in his hand and murmured, 'Good, very good, we can use that.'

Some of my own words by-lined from the London Office appeared next day in 'one of the world's great newspapers'.

After a fortnight in a dreary London hotel and working in an even drearier near-empty office I cheerfully caught the train and steamed back north. York Station looked welcoming and almost cosy after the cavern-like, dead-end abruptness of Kings Cross. The Minster was peeping over the medieval walls and the green ramparts had a sprinkling of gold as the first daffodils lifted their heads. I was glad to be home. It only vaguely occurred to me that down in London there had perhaps been yet another path not taken. What if I had shown more enthusiasm for Fleet Street? What if I had pleaded with the Great Man to let me stay? What then? A career in the famous Street? Wait a moment. Think again. Upheaval! Moving house, daughter moving school! Did I want that? Here I was again back in ambition's graveyard and contented to be here. I decided to stop brooding and finish that second book.

37

Most of us were belligerent members of the National Union of Journalists — belligerent because the union head office in London was always threatening to call us out on strike and we did not want to go. Strikes were fashionable. The whole country was striking or talking about striking and there were even comedy shows on television about them. 'Everybody out!' was a popular catch phrase.

Society seemed to be at war with itself and then a union crisis arose locally. A freelance journalist appeared in the city brandishing an NUJ card and demanding that the cosy arrangement with Noel Blenkin, our local war hero should cease forthwith. We should not be supporting someone who was not a member of the union, he declared.

Noel was a member of the Institute of Journalists, a much more sedate organisation, but this had not bothered the local reporting fraternity. Noel was Noel and he was getting on a bit; he needed support. Angry union meetings were held in the upstairs room of a pub hired free on condition the bar downstairs was put to good use. No solution was found. The union head office backed the new freelance and threatened excommunication for anyone guilty of helping our war hero. An irritating, and disturbingly efficient freelance entered our cosy little news-gathering world, someone who was not going to share his scoops with anyone. From now on we dreaded the early morning phone calls:

'Have you seen the story in the Daily Express? What are you lot doing over there? How did you miss that?'

We would all have to sharpen up our ideas, change our ways, perhaps even change our ideas about what was news but there remained the problem of Noel. Being the gentleman he was he solved the problem himself — he gave up freelancing except for football reporting and became a full-time court shorthand-writer instead. And we learned to live with the competition of a freelance splashing about in what we had regarded as our own exclusive little pool.

And then the union struck again and we too were called out on strike. I had always thought grandly that our staff was above that sort of thing. There had been the usual weasel-worded ballot — 'if your negotiating committee feel that deadlock has been reached then the executive has the authority to call a strike forthwith.'

Protests that striking should be the subject of a second ballot were always met with the same response: 'you cannot negotiate without the backing of a strike commitment.' Tabloid colour was often added by saying: 'Without a commitment to strike you are walking into the negotiating room naked'.

So suddenly we were on strike. We comforted ourselves by saying it would soon be over but the paper continued to appear without us. Those die-hards of the union world, the printers, had a golden rule: never cross a picket line. When they went on strike the newspaper world froze but when journalists stopped work the printers walked straight through their picket lines and worked as usual. The Editor turned out a newspaper of sorts all by himself and as the strike dragged on it was clear that the only people suffering were the journalists. No money was coming in but money was going out. The mortgage had to be paid and we had to eat.

Colleague Keith had four children to feed and got himself a job in the station hotel. The manager, a kindly soul, told him they had never had such a meticulous 'washer-upperer' despite being hugely overqualified for the job with his Cambridge degree.

We ate out of the deep freeze. Meriel had always been a Squirrel Nutkin and for weeks the only food she bought was milk. She made bulk quantities of soup with vegetables from the garden so when the deep freeze emptied we could keep going with our own soup kitchen. I did odd jobs around the house but with a growing feeling of guilt; by striking I was deliberately creating hardship for my family. I humbly visited the manager of our building society and explained the problem.

'Would it help,' he said, 'if we suspended your monthly payments for a while?'

'That would be extremely helpful,' I said.

We shook hands.

What a nice man. Perhaps being a journalist on a great newspaper did have some status after all even if it was on strike. Even daughter Penny was suffering but doing so stoically. She wrote to her grandma in Wales.

Dad is on strike and mum says we can't afford any more sweets so I am going to save my Mars bar in case I get really really hungry.

My parents gave us some money so we could tax the car and at least keep mobile. I used the mobility to travel to Leeds for a mass meeting of staff called to report progress, but of course there was no progress. At home Meriel had silently listened to me protesting about the stupidity of it all. It was a ridiculous situation because we were not on strike for ourselves at all. We had already been offered a salary increase above what the NUJ was demanding. We were on strike for our less fortunate brothers on other newspapers. This was very noble but with the domestic bills mounting such altruism was wearing thin. Meriel listened to my moans with mounting irritation.

'It's no good going on to me about it,' she said. 'Do something about it — tell *them* it's stupid, not me.'

So I did. I pushed my way forward in a crowded dance hall at Leeds, a room hired for the occasion and seething with people, and I let fly. I was astonished at the sound of my own voice ringing out. I was astonished at my own eloquence. Who was this man that everyone was staring at?

There were loud murmurs of support but also loud murmurs of anger. We should call this off now, I said, in full rhetorical mode. To my complete astonishment I forced a ballot, a formal affair with people queuing up with their bits of paper. People were now looking at me very oddly and I was not surprised. They regarded me as some John the Baptist figure appearing out of the wilderness of a district office and wailing woe and disaster. I awaited the result of the ballot in hope and trepidation — hope that I might end the strike and trepidation that in the process I could seriously damage a powerful union.

By a narrow majority the mass meeting voted that the strike should continue but the decision left no-one happy; it had shown how deeply divided people were. But now a highly respected assistant editor was on his feet and we all listened and hoped for guidance.

'The NUJ,' he said, 'should take warning from this vote. The union has put us in this situation and sadly we now have no choice but to see it through to the end. However . . . ' And his pause was dramatic.

'As soon as this strike is over,' he said, 'I intend resigning from this union and I invite others who feel the same way to join me.'

Shouts of 'hear hear' were only partially drowned by shouts of 'no, no!'

The meeting broke up with nothing resolved but for me there was a strange sense of achievement. I had let off steam and the vote had given other people some satisfaction too; we had failed but only narrowly.

'I really told them,' I said to Meriel.

'So when are you going back? When do we start getting some money again?'

I had come home elated but of course nothing had changed.

'It can't last much longer.'

'Hah!' she said.

In fact it went on for eleven weeks and the deep freezer was nearly empty before it was resolved. When we did return to work we discovered that legally we should not be paid for another month. But then out of the blue we all received a cheque for one hundred pounds. The covering letter from the management explained:

'This is an advance of salary to help out after the recent difficulties.'

We were solvent again. Keith hung up his dish cloth in the station hotel and received a personal thank-you letter from the manager. Life returned to normal and we all decided that perhaps after all we were employed by one of the world's 'great newspapers'.

38

Strange to be back at work trying to find out what we had missed during those eleven weeks. We liked to think that people had missed us but it was not apparent. The world had gone on as usual. I scurried round my usual haunts trying to catch up. The archaeologists were still digging underneath the Minster and the builders were at their elbows waiting to pour concrete. It was a constant battle — the archaeologists demanding more time to examine the foundations of even older churches and the builders anxious to keep the repair work on schedule. But even they were impressed when the burrowing archaeologists came across huge drums of stone which came from the columns of the Roman forum that pre-dated all the churches on the site. The harassed archaeologists had one little triumph when the builders poured molten concrete into a tiny hole to fill up what they thought was a small void under the foundations but they had to go on pouring and pouring.

'Why didn't you ask?' said the archaeologists. 'You are filling up an old well.'

It was not immediately apparent but alongside the birth pangs of tourism the city was facing a deluge of archaeology. York could not escape the growing national pressure for redevelopment. When developers cleared areas for rebuilding in the city centre beneath them lay layers of continuous history going back nearly 2000 years — it was an archaeologist's dream. A flurry of 'rescue digs' broke out as archaeologists explored and recorded ahead of the builders, archaeology was suddenly news and the specialist world which I had had to myself was invaded by 'the media'.

This came home to me when builders strengthening the foundations of a city centre shop suddenly dropped into a stone-lined tunnel. It was part of a massive Roman sewer system big enough to walk through as long as you kept your head down. The archaeologists were soon off tunnelling under the streets of the city like eager moles clearing away the dubious silt of ages even finding jewellery that some careless Roman had dropped down the loo. Press and VIP visits were organised, electric lights were installed and the underground world attracted a stream of distinguished visitors including a prince and an Archbishop. And there was more — an old sweet factory in the heart of the city was demolished and a vast site was cleared for redevelopment; the archaeologists moved in en masse. It looked promising, they said.

My obsession with history meanwhile had not gone unnoticed by the features department who wanted to fill the week-end supplements.

'How about a series of historical newspapers?' said the editor? 'Pick a big day in the city's history and produce a two-page tabloid as if printed on the day.'

I was back in the past again. We brought out a newspaper dated just after the battle of Marston Moor when the Royalist survivors streamed back to York only to be locked out.

We 'reported' on the disgrace of George Hudson, the Railway King, who invented the first Ponzi financial scandal — using investors' money to pay huge 'dividends' to later investors. But my favourite was the report on King Harold slaughtering the invading Vikings at Stamford Bridge near York in 1066. Headline news gave a gory account of the battle and how the pitiful survivors were allowed to sail back to Norway to tell the fearful tale of what happened to people who invaded England. The paper had a Stop Press column into which I slipped a news flash:

William, Duke of Normandy lands at Hastings with a huge army.

I was very proud of this until I reflected: why was I congratulating myself on a scoop a thousand years after the event?

★　★　★

In the office we were having smoke problems. George favoured cigars and Jim had his pipe. Jim was a former subeditor from Leeds who lived near our office. He had not been well and disliked travelling so he was transferred to us. Rarely did he leave the office so the pipe burned continuously. His whole day was a smoke-filled ritual and not a breath he drew was nicotine free. He would refill his pipe and apply a match without taking his eyes off the piece of paper on which he was working. The spent match would be neatly laid on the mounting pile his ash tray. George's contributions to this air-less smoke-zone were sporadic but even more intense. Blue cigar smoke would hang in layers across the room. When his cigar was drawing well we qualified to be included in the daily shipping forecasts — the ones that warned of 'poor visibility'.

I pleaded with head office and we had an extractor fan installed. At full blast one could see the blue haze rushing towards the fan like a poltergeist eager to escape a ghost-hunter. It was not a healthy environment in which to work and tragically so it was to prove.

★   ★   ★

If it were possible to have a routine in an office where one was at the whim of the next telephone call I would escape for fresh air and a mid-morning coffee with Stacey, a reporter friend on the local paper. Although on different newspapers we had worked together for years reporting the same dinners, council meetings, fires and accidents. We were friends, not rivals and our fields of work interest fortunately did not clash — he revelled in the pop world having been a radio disc jockey in Italy during his National Service while I wallowed in history.

We would sit in the splendour of Terry's tea-room surrounded by polished mahogany panelling salvaged from some ocean liner and discuss the world, our world and our daily attempts to explain its activities to our readers. It was the one civilised smoke-free moment of the day. We were middle-aged now and settled into a rut, writing stories that were disturbingly familiar about annual even triennial events. Don't let your rut become your grave some morbid wag once said. Easier said than done particularly if it was a comfortable rut.

The royalty cheque for the book arrived — £400 — for a year's work! I could have earned more money talking to the Women's Institutes. Authorship was not a life changing experience after all, and in a curt letter Longmans succinctly explained why my second book would never see a library shelf. My spirits were at low ebb. Fortunately another distraction was at hand.

39

There arrived on the desk another invitation from the army. Would I like to visit a regiment manning a far-flung outpost of the former British Empire in Belize? I had to look it up in the Atlas. It was a tiny country on the strip of land joining the north and south Americas and just north of the Panama Canal. What on earth was the British army doing over there in America's backyard?

As soon as head office discovered that the RAF was providing transport free of charge the trip was approved. I retreated to the Reference Library for a history lesson and some climate information. Belize was a few miles north of the Panama Canal where thousands of construction workers had died of Yellow Fever. This was going to be fun.

*　*　*

Two of us were standing on the runway at RAF Brize Norton looking apprehensively at a huge four-engine transport aircraft. My companion was Peter, a reporter from the local paper, a public schoolboy with ambitions to become a war correspondent. The aircraft was a Hercules and totally unlike the sleek jets I had seen at Heathrow; this aircraft was brutally functional and there was not an air hostess in sight. The rear section of the plane was lowered like a medieval drawbridge and a figure in overalls with three stripes on his sleeve beckoned us inside with our suitcases. The cavernous interior was filled with huge crates fastened down with khaki belts and the sergeant indicated the seating along the sides — seating made of metal tubes and still more khaki belts.

'Make yourselves comfortable,' he said. Another figure joined us wearing army fatigues and a major's crown on his shoulder. The briefest of nods and he slung his kit underneath the seat opposite us. The sergeant squeezed past the crates and climbed a vertical ladder onto the flight deck. A few minutes later he returned.

'Emergency instructions,' he said. 'Listen up. In the event of us landing on water you climb up this ladder and go out through the hatch just above my head. Then you walk along the wing to your right,' he helpfully pointed, 'and when you get to the wing tip you will find me waiting for you with a little rubber dinghy equipped with flares, paddles and lots of sweeties'.

That all seemed quite straightforward but what if we landed in a howling gale and amidst crashing waves? Would we ever reach the little dinghy and the promised sweeties? I decided it was best not to think about such things.

'Right!' said the sergeant. 'We're closing up.'

The great drawbridge slowly started to rise and clanged shut, sealing us into this dark metal box. Our backs were pressed uncomfortably against to the aircraft's sides and the towering package cases were like a wall a few feet from our faces. I fought off claustrophobia as the engines coughed and spluttered and the whole aircraft shook. Ear-defenders were distributed.

'That's just the two inner engines,' shouted the sergeant. 'Wait until they're all going.'

And when they did the noise was hellish so loud it drove all thoughts out of your head and left you breathless. The major was reading a book.

'How long?' I mouthed at the sergeant. He held up eight fingers. Eight hours in this roaring, rattling nightmare!

We took off with the engines screaming and after a while the sergeant was back at the top of the ladder and beckoning us to join him. Up in the cabin the pilots nodded to us and pointed at the glowing horizon. We had taken off just after dusk, but as our aircraft climbed the sun slowly came back up again. We watched fascinated — the sun was going backwards. We reached cruising height.

'Try and get some shuteye,' one of the pilots shouted above the noise before adding: 'if you can'.

We returned to the cargo hold where the major was already stretched out asleep. I marvelled at his composure but I had more immediate concerns. In dumb show I explained my needs to the sergeant and he pointed to a corner behind the crates. I squeezed past the huge boxs and found a chemical toilet bolted to the floor in full view of anyone on their way to the flight deck.

After eight hours of unspeakable, mind-numbing noise we landed in Bermuda — a pit stop on our journey to Central America. The engines stopped and the silence was so profound that I thought I had gone deaf. The drawbridge slowly descended and a blast of hot moist air came out of the inky darkness and almost took our breath away. As the drawbridge struck the floor a figure appeared out of the blackness dressed immaculately in a white uniform and wearing a peaked white cap glistening with gold trimmings. He was like a character from a Ruritanean operetta and in his pristine presence we felt like prisoners released from a scruffy dungeon.

'Good evening gentlemen,' he said, 'welcome to Bermuda.' And he saluted. Dirty, tired and sweaty as I was I didn't feel we deserved such courtesies. A car was waiting for us with a driver and a captain from what I learned was the Bermuda Territorial Army. We were to be their overnight guests in the local barracks and a dinner had been arranged. It was dark and I stared through the car windows wanting to see more of Bermuda but only caught glimpses of idyllic white stone houses with exotic gardens.

The captain was a solicitor when not a soldier and he entertained us royally. Our major who was clearly more used to long-distance travel than we were, disappeared into the toilets and returned looking spruce and freshly shaven. We realised too late that both Peter and I went into dine with five o'clock shadows. Our host was affable and eager to talk as dinner was awaited in the mess and I wanted to know more about life on this little dot of an island in the middle of the Atlantic Ocean.

'It must be like living in paradise,' I said.

'More like hell sometimes,' said our host as dinner was served. 'You're living on top of each other here — you know everybody and they all know you. You can't get away from them. There's nowhere else to go'.

So even Paradise had its drawback.

'Right,' said the captain when the coffee cups had been drained. 'Nice warm evening. Let's go for a swim.'

We were all taken slightly aback.

'Love to,' said Peter 'but my costume is in my case on the aircraft.'

'You don't need costumes,' said the captain. 'Steward! Get us some towels'.

Nude bathing? I imaged the headlines in the local Bermuda News: 'Journalists and soldiers in nude bathing scandal.' But perhaps it was a private pool so it would not matter. But as we drove out of the town I realised I was wrong. We travelled in bright moonlight until we reached sand dunes and a scattering of trees and bushes. The car stopped.

'Follow me but mind those bushes,' called the officer. 'They're bloody sharp — Don't call them Portugese bayonets for nothing.'

We picked our way through the sand dunes and we were on a beach, soft, warm sand squidging under foot. The waves were turning over in long white lines in the moonlight.

'Come on,' said our host who was already stripping off. I saw his white buttocks galloping off towards the water. Perhaps this was what they did in Bermuda. We followed, all of us naked, but memories of chilly bathing in Cornwall stopped me at the water's edge. This sea however was different, my feet felt as if I were going into a warm bath. We romped and splashed in the eerie moonlight like silly school children.

Next morning we saw the island in daylight and it sparkled. We drove back to the airport, past picture-postcard houses and harbours with yachts parked in never-ending rows — it was upper class suburbia with sails and sunshine and we saw a policeman in his English uniform and smartly-pressed Bermuda shorts. But this world was not for us. The gaping mouth of the Hercules swallowed us up and we growled our way to Belize.

40

On the last leg of our journey I got to know a little more about my fellow reporter, Peter. He was in his early twenties and if he could not be a war correspondent he would settle for being a defence correspondent on one of the national broadsheets. He achieved his ambition and much later I read his authoritative articles with envy.

Our pilot took a good look at the airport in Belize before he put the aircraft down; he explained that he did not like runways that were built on swamps especially when flying a heavily laden aircraft. We touched down and the Hercules came to a standstill, the drawbridge was lowered and we were hit in the face with a gush of bathwater-warm air. We were in the tropics surrounded by swamp and forest. It was not just the heat that was discomforting — the air felt wet.

A captain in smart tropical kit was waiting for us and I tried not to stare at the incongruous plastic cover on his nose. Sitting alongside him in his jeep while sweating profusely and finding it difficult to breathe I could examine the nose more carefully. It was not a grand Cyrano de Bergerac but a carefully moulded piece of skin-coloured plastic held in place with a thin strand of elastic round his head. The captain tapped the plastic nose with his finger nail.

'Nasty skin infection,' he said. 'Got to keep the sun off it or it won't heal. Dentist made this for me out of the stuff that holds false teeth together. Brilliant eh!'

He drummed his fingers on his plastic nose. So that was one little mystery solved.

'Got to make a detour into town,' said the captain. 'Must introduce you to the local administrator. Independent country now you see. Observe protocol and all that. We're only guests and he knows a flight's come in. Only polite to tell him who's visiting'.

Our officer led the way into the big white, air-conditioned colonial style office, striding through a room full of women secretaries: 'No giggling!' he ordered very loudly but they did. We met and shook hands with the local administrator who didn't know what to say to us nor we to him. The captain completely uninhibited by his plastic nose explained how we were going to write articles about the British soldiers for the benefit of their families back home.

'Enjoy your visit,' were the only words the administrator uttered. We left his cool office, strode back through the still giggling secretaries and outside into the sticky wet heat and boarded our Jeep.

The Union Jack was flying proudly over the army camp and we reached the welcome sanctuary of the air-conditioned cool of the officers' mess. This was a large wooden building with shabby easy chairs, a picture of the Queen on the wall and a cupboard with a selection of the regimental silver. Our suitcases were whisked away and the colonel appeared to give us a brisk briefing.

I found the history fascinating. Once the haunt of pirates, the country had fallen to the British who saw a chance to exploit its valuable mahogany. Eventually what had been British Honduras gained its independence and became Belize. Its neighbour Guatemala, however, was not friendly and coveted the territory because of its access to the sea. Fearing an invasion, the new rulers of Belize asked the British army to stay — just in case. This explained why some 1500 British troops were out here sweating in the heat and acquiring a sun tan.

'We've got a great programme worked out for you,' said the colonel. 'Bit of fishing, bit of jungle bashing. You're under canvas by the way but we'll make sure the bugs don't bite. Use the mess here as your base. You'll soon get used to the heat'.

That I doubted and I did not like the idea of being under canvas in this climate. A young lieutenant took us to our sleeping quarters. It was a small marquee and as we arrived an alien-like figure in a gas mask with a pack on his back stepped out through the tent flap holding a tube belching grey smoke. Seeing us coming he turned off a knob on his back-pack and the tube stopped smoking. He removed his gas mask revealing a very young sweaty face.

'Give it a minute. It's a bit thick in there,' he said.

We waited and watched grey smoke curling out from under tent flaps and the air vents on the roof. The young lieutenant took the waiting-time as an opportunity to give us some advice.

'Make sure you use the mosquito nets and there's a can of insecticide by the bed. Put your shoes on top of the locker not on the floor and make sure you tap them out before you put your foot in them in the morning.'

I was getting increasingly nervous particularly as our marquee was still gently billowing smoke.

'One more thing,' said the lieutenant. 'There's a nasty little snake called a Lance de Feu, about a foot long. Not seen one in camp yet but if you do see one give it a wide berth.'

My nervousness increased as we followed the lieutenant into our quarters. There were two beds with mosquito nets and two wooden cupboards with our suitcases already standing alongside them. Grey smoke still hung in the air and the smell of insecticide stung the nostrils. But what disturbed me more were the death throes of an entire insect population; scores of flies were spinning wildly on the top of the cupboard, while moths and various butterflies were flapping feebly on the groundsheets. We were in a gas chamber. At least we had electricity: two light bulbs controlled by a switch mounted on a bit of board hung on a string near the entrance.

'Toilets et cetera in the mess,' said the lieutenant. 'Torches in the cupboard, you'll need them. And jacket and tie for dinner please.'

Jacket and tie for dinner! In this heat! We were left to make ourselves at home.

'Oh my God!' was Peter's only comment.

Dusk fell at an alarming speed. One moment there was bright sunlight and then the sun was gone, no gentle twilight, suddenly it was dark, frighteningly dark in our tent. Putting on the lights did not make it any more homely as we dressed for dinner. Outside looked forbiddingly black with just the distant glow of lights in the officers' mess offering a distant glimpse of civilisation as we knew it. We found our torches and stepped outside only to be disturbed yet again by the startling and unreal combination of darkness and heat. We followed a concrete path through other tents towards the mess. Every few yards along the path there were posts standing about three foot high from which were suspended fire buckets; I had not noticed them in the daylight. As we approached something moved on the top of one of the posts and there was a vicious snapping sound. I nearly leapt out of my skin. Our torches picked out a large crab balanced on top of the post and it was snapping its claws at us. Nearly every post had an angry resident. Crabs? How could there be crabs? We expressed our alarm to the corporal behind the bar in the mess.

'Land crabs, sir. They're after the water in the buckets. Vicious things if you tread on them.'

We had a lively, and entertaining dinner with the officers wanting our views on the election campaign going on at home. We tried to turn the conversation to the value or otherwise of having British troops out in this last fragment of the former British Empire but to no avail; they had been well-briefed about the dangers of being too expansive with journalists.

'Fishing's good,' was the laconic reply accompanied by laughter and meaningful looks. One of the company was in full regimental dress and glowing gently despite the air conditioning. I quietly asked him why.

'Duty officer,' he whispered. 'Always full regimentals if we have guests. Colonel's orders.'

I felt guilty — every night during our stay some poor duty officer had to get dressed up and sit hot and uncomfortable all through dinner. It was an enjoyable evening — a little piece of England firmly entrenched in a foreign field.

We made our way back to the marquee and this time the land crabs were on the move, scuttling ahead of us and looking grotesque in the torch light. We found the switch for our bedroom lights and in their dim glow the net-draped beds looked sinister and uninviting. We discovered that after the earlier chemical attack the insect life of Belize had regrouped. Our two light bulbs were surrounded by a buzzing haze of insects which slowly grew larger and larger. Peter and I seized our aerosol sprays and let fly. It rained corpses, many of them tumbling down the sides of the mosquito nets. Unwillingly we got undressed and climbed into our respective beds carefully tucking in the nets under the mattress. We both sat up, sprays at the ready waiting to mop up anything that might have sneaked inside the nets with us. As I was stretching out to put the spray-can on the bedside table Peter said: 'We've forgotten to put the bloody light out.'

It was a very brief argument because I was clearly the closest but having crept back to bed by torch-light I got my own back.

'You've left your shoes on the floor,' I said. 'There'll be a snake nesting in them in the morning.'

Grumblings and curses followed. We tried to settle for the night but we were assailed by strange chirrupings and scratching; a warm breeze flapped the canvas reminding us how close we were to the creepy-crawly world outside. I lay and shivered despite the heat — if those land crabs could climb up fire posts what was to stop them climbing into bed with me?

In the half light I saw something that made my heart thump: a strangely shaped shadow was on the roof of the tent and it was moving. I grabbed the torch and switched it on. The 'thing' was not on top of the tent at all it was inside. Some sort of lizard that must have had sucker pads for feet was walking slowly across the tent ceiling upside down. I watched as it slowly walked above me and down the far tent wall. Once on the ground however it moved at surprising speed and disappeared out under the canvas. I switched off my torch, closed my eyes, and thought of England.

41

The colonel was right — he did have a busy programme for us. With the young lieutenant as our guide, we went off by jeep meeting groups of soldiers guarding the airfield and occupying deeply camouflaged strong points near important river crossings deep in the hot damp forests. The grand plan, we were told, was for the garrison to guard the airfield so British reinforcements could be rushed in by air to repel unwanted visitors. The young squaddies from Leeds and Bradford were not much concerned about the grand strategy — for them this was an exciting exotic location with spells of living rough out in the jungle alternating with rest and recreation on a hot beach beside a warm sea.

After a day of interviews, we too were promised some rest and recreation — sea fishing. A boat was hired and we were joined by the major we had met on the Hercules; he was to be the fisherman. The harbour was filled with small boats tied to wooden jetties and still more fastened to mooring posts set in rows out in the harbour; nearly every post had a pelican perched on it, ridiculous awkward-looking birds that stared at us as with as much curiosity as we stared at them.

The sun beat down, the water sparkled and shimmered, the craft nodded lazily at their moorings against a background of unpainted and dilapidated wooden sheds. It was a tropical setting for a James Bond movie, but sadly without high-powered speed boats or pretty girls.

We boarded our tiny craft with its miniscule cabin and chugged out of the harbour into an eerily flat shallow sea. I was sitting near the prow looking down into the crystal clear water. Suddenly there was turmoil in the water ahead of us and a giant stingray shook itself free of the sandy sea bed and flapped its way ahead of us. I shouted excitedly and the two other passengers crowded forward to watch. On we sailed, the heat intensified and the shore was just a distant smear on the horizon; the sea however was still only a few feet deep.

The major busied himself with his fishing tackle including a rod that looked more like a pole and the line which appeared to be made of wire.

'We're going out to the reef,' he said. 'That's why this damn place was never developed — ships can't get in — the shallow water goes out for miles.'

The boatman slowed the engine and he and the major had a conversation. An anchor was thrown out.

'You guys want a swim this is the place to do it,' said the major. True leader of men that he was he stripped off and jumped in. He stood up in the sea demonstrating that it was only chest deep. We joined him and started swimming round and round the boat. The water was silkily warm but where was the land. At water level it had disappeared completely. If something happened to the boat which way did I swim ashore, or in my case — walk?

While we swam the boatman set out lunch, and then I saw him climbing the mast. He reached the cross-tree near the top, wrapped his legs around it and sat there. Strange place for sunbathing I thought or was he checking which way the land lay for the return journey? The major surged past me doing a sturdy breast stroke.

'What's he up to?' I asked pointing. The major rolled expertly onto his back to take a look.

'Sharks probably,' he said. 'Just keeping an eye open'.

And off he went for another circuit of the boat. At the mention of sharks I decided it was time for lunch and so did Peter. We ate sandwiches and emptied copious cans of lemonade before the boat reached the edge of the reef. Here the friendly, shallow sea gave way abruptly to dark, deep, and sinister depths. The major eagerly got out his fishing pole, opened a sealed bucket of revolting bait, and started fishing. He just sat there with a huge hat keeping off the glare of the sun. Peter and I retreated into the shade of the tiny cabin and as the time ticked by the heat rose. The boat rocked gently and the boatman had a siesta.

'I don't get this,' said Peter. 'It's so boring! If you're fly-fishing you at least get to see the damn fish, but this . . . Look at him.'

The major was sitting hunched under his big floppy hat and slowly marinating in full sun. Then he stirred.

'I say, one of you chaps. Just hold this rod for a minute will you. I need a drink.'

Peter refused to move so I volunteered. The heavy rod was thrust into my hand and the major retreated into the shadow of the cabin; the sun turned all its fierce intentions on me. No sooner had the major gone than the rod almost leapt out of my hand and the reel screamed as the wire raced out. I tried to grab the winding handle but it was twirling so fast it nearly took my fingers off.

'Hey! Hey!' I shouted for I needed help.

The major threw aside his can of coke and was alongside me in seconds shouting instructions. The tugging on the line was violent.

'Take it!' I shouted.

'It's your fish!' he shouted.

'You can have it,' I shouted. 'I can't hold it!'

He grabbed the rod out of my heads, sat back and braced his legs against the bulwark of the boat. Clearly a professional was at work here. The boatman had quietly joined us with a huge fishing net. After much winding and heaving the fish appeared and to my amateur eyes it looked twice the size of any fish that I had ever seen on a fishmonger's slab. The major was trembling with excitement.

'Your fish,' he said to me producing a camera and taking photographs. I watched the beautiful thing gasping its last and willingly renounced all claim. Enthusiastically the major re-baited the hook and starting fishing again. Peter and I exchanged glances — we were in for another serious session of hot sticky boredom. But the boatman came to our rescue. He left his post by the engine and addressed us.

'He,' he said pointing at me, 'he is da lucky man. Always on da boat d'ere is one lucky man, and he is dat man. Give him da rod and there'll be another fish.'

The major laughed.

'OK. It's all yours. And this time you land it yourself.'

I was back in the sun and it happened again, a violent jerk on the line, the wire racing and my arms nearly being wrenched out of their sockets. In all physical endeavours I had long since realised that I was built for speed not strength. I was more whippet than bulldog and besides I knew nothing about the techniques for landing big fish.

'It's all yours,' I shouted. 'I don't know how to land the damn thing'.

Without protest the major grabbed back the rod and an astonishing fight followed. The boatman was standing on the deck-rail holding onto the rigging watching the taught line as it zigzagged through the water. The major skilfully reeled in and occasionally released the line as the fish fought furiously for its life. There was a flash of silver and a shape momentarily broke the surface.

'Barracuda!' shouted the boatman. 'Barracuda! Front of boat, front of boat!' and he waved at us frantically to go to the prow. He dived into the cabin and brought out a wooden club while the major continued heaving and winding; the boatman joined him club in hand and peered over the side. We cowered in the prow wondering what sort of monster was going to be brought aboard. A Herculean heave by the major and the fish came partly over the side; it was huge and it had teeth; after more heaving the barracuda was in the boat, thrashing wildly, slithering and snapping. It took three blows from the club before it was still and then I felt sorry for the beautiful thing. Why was it necessary to inflict such violence on a poor fish but then I examined its teeth more closely: even in its death throes they could have caused a nasty injury. The major was in ecstasy. He was going to have it preserved and stuffed.

'Are you sure you don't want it?' he kept asking me.

The boatman meanwhile was pointing at me and grinning.

'Da lucky man,' he said. 'I said he was da lucky man'.

The fishing expedition was the talk of the mess that evening and common sense prevailed with the major. He abandoned the idea of taking a stuffed barracuda back to England and the boatman and his family and probably his neighbours had a fish supper instead.

★　★　★

On our last night the young lieutenant decided to show us the night life. We had wondered what the young soldiers did for social entertainment but were too nervous to ask. With the lieutenant in civilian clothes we joined a raucous bus load of noisy young men and went into town and de-bussed by a large, dilapidated wooden building ablaze with lights; music was blaring inside. The lieutenant gave us some local money to buy drinks.

'I've got a couple of errands to run,' he said. 'I'll join you in about ten minutes. Talk to some of the lads, but don't believe half what they tell you.'

It was a dance hall with two big fans slowly revolving in the ceiling. A disc jockey was up on the stage and the music was deafening. Our squaddies were soon on the floor with partners and dancing with cumbersome expertise. The women were all dressed in brightly coloured party frocks, all small in stature and to my critical eye there was not a pretty one in sight.

'Oh Gawd, just look at them,' said Peter.

The seating on the left hand side of the hall had been left strangely empty so that was where we sat; the squaddies we thought having more exciting things on their mind than being interviewed. We watched and marvelled as an incredible parade of dancers clomped by. But now we were being eyed by a group of women sitting by the stage and in whom the soldiers were taking no interest at all.

'I think someone fancies you,' said Peter. 'Look out they're coming over. It must be a ladies' excuse me or something. Now what do we do?'

Two women sat down one on either side of us, crossing their legs, smoothing down their skirts and adjusting the top of their off-the-shoulder dresses a fraction downwards to reveal a little more cleavage.

'You want?' said the lady sitting next to me.

'To dance?' I said pointing at the dancers.

She looked puzzled and shook her head.

'You want?' she repeated.

I overheard Peter having a similar type of conversation.

'Why are you sitting on this side of the hall?'

It was the voice of our lieutenant.

'It was the only place where we could sit,' said Peter.

'You're confusing the natives,' said the lieutenant. 'Dance partners to the right and the 'you-know-what's' to the left.'

He said something to the two women and they stood up completely expressionless, mine trailing her fingers down the length of my arm before she departed.

'They were a bit surprised getting customers so early on,' said the lieutenant. 'People don't usually move over to their side until they've had a few. Have you fed the fish yet?'

It was an abrupt change of conversation but we followed our saviour to the other side of the hall picking our way through the jiggling dancers. The lieutenant pulled on a cord and a roller blind went upwards. Cool air curled in from the darkness. We were on a veranda suspended over the river and below us was a powerful lamp shining down on the dark water beneath us.

'Wait one,' said the lieutenant and within minutes he was back from the food counter with a sandwich.

'Chuck that in.'

We did and the water boiled with churning silver fish.

'They eat anything,' said our guide. 'And I do mean anything.'

We did our duty by mingling with the soldiery and discovered that our brief encounter with the local ladies on the professional side of the dance hall had caused much amusement.

One slightly tipsy squaddie told us: 'After you've been here a couple of months some of them don't look at all bad.'

The journey back on the camp bus was even more raucous than the journey out.

★   ★   ★

Next day we thanked the colonel and the others for their hospitality and returned to the noisy womb of our Hercules. This time we refuelled in the Azores before landing at Brize Norton, deaf and dazed, and just in time to miss the last train home. We spent the night in a bleak RAF barrack room but at least there was nothing sinister crawling across the ceiling. I returned knowing a great deal about Belize and barrier reefs, big game fishing and Central American politics. Meriel however was not impressed.

'I've never known anyone with as much useless knowledge as you have.'

And she was right. Jack of all trades and master of none, that was me, just like the other members of my so-called profession.

42

After experiencing jungle nights, snapping land crabs and thrashing barracudas it was difficult to get back into the office routine; it all seemed so parochial and boring.

'How dare you say you're bored,' cried Meriel. 'Some people spend their whole life looking at the same four walls of an office. Think yourself lucky.'

She was right of course but what was I achieving of any permanence and importance? Here I was chasing stories, rushing them into print and then it was all over — gone! It was true what they said: today's scoop wrapped up tomorrow's fish and chips and now even chip shops were discarding newspapers in favour of plastic cartons. It was all so transient.

'That archaeologist chap has been chasing you,' said Keith breaking into one of my midlife crisis moods. 'Said it was important.'

So I stopped moping and went off on my favourite activity — looking at holes in the ground. The old sweet factory which had made a famous brand of sugared almonds had been cleared down to the bare soil in preparation for a new street of shops. The great gap in the town centre was hidden from hurrying office workers by large wooden hoardings. Behind the screens even I was astonished and I was used to visiting archaeological sites. It was a vast excavation, holes and trenches everywhere with board-walks picking paths between them and scores of students in jeans and floppy hats crouched hard at work.

Richard, a veteran of scores of digs in the city, was in a Portakabin stacked with maps and boxes of pottery. He was excited, a Viking town was being unearthed, he said, and the damp, peaty soil had preserved wood, leather and even fabric. The wooden walls of houses were being uncovered complete with the rushes on the floor and the wattle fencing surround-ing the house gardens. Forget the old image of rapers and pillagers, these were the homes of Vikings who had become settlers, traders and craftsmen even if their leader bore the unfriendly name of Eric Bloodaxe.

Richard's enthusiasm was infectious. Once again a muddy hole in the ground was making news, big news, and the archaeolo-gists knew how to arouse public interest. A stream of Nordic royalty paid visits to marvel at the discovery of one of their far-flung outposts; once upon a time the Vikings, not the British, had been the world's adventurers and conquerors. With this latest archaeological discovery added to the ongoing repairs to the cathedral and the royal wedding, the city was becoming more and more an attraction for tourists but we, the local journalists, were losing our pre-eminence as the city's main news gatherers and observers. Local television had arrived and many of us felt the writing, or rather the picture, was on the wall. The public was agog with excitement. Seeing it on 'telly' was so much more exciting than seeing a photograph and a report in the local newspaper. What could I do to assuage these attacks of not too divine discontent?

Penny had been taking A levels and this gave me an idea. Those blank spots on job application forms had always embarrassed me so why not take a few A levels myself — it would give me something worthwhile to do and stop me brooding. So I went to night-school once a week and started my education all over again. Soon Penny was packing to go to university and looking miserable about the prospect. Our only chick was leaving the nest. Meriel appeared composed and brisk and I was unconvincingly cheerful.

'You'll have a great time. Best years of your life.'

More practically I added: 'And you're not

too far away if you want to pay us a visit.'

With the car packed I disappeared into the toilet and had a quiet weep. I was losing my only child, the little soul I had dragged around castles and earthworks and archaeological digs and fatally infected with a love of history. Not much was said on the journey to university and not much more was said as we drove back home without her.

'She'll be all right,' said Meriel.

'Of course she will.'

★   ★   ★

Mother and father abandoned Wales and came to live near us but the long arm of *hiraeth* reached out when father died. We took mother back to Wales with a grey metal urn in a cardboard box packed amid the suitcases in the car boot. A very small group of us stood in the grave-yard of Deugorn Denio under umbrellas as prayers were intoned in Welsh and English. When we went back to the hotel mother said:

'Poor John.'

'Why poor me?' I asked although I knew the answer. 'Because you are going to have to make this same journey for me, aren't you?'

<h1 style="text-align:center">43</h1>

Now the Government was at war with the miners. The Sixties might have been swinging but we were now in the Striking Seventies. The 'I'm backing Britain' campaign launched with such patriotic fervour had petered out and the country's mood had changed. National self-confidence was replaced with dissatisfied belligerence against everyone and everything. Police and protesters clashed outside the American Embassy in London. What was the matter with the world? The camaraderie and social togetherness of the immediate post-war years had been frittered away.

'The workers' had decided that there was an old enemy to fight — the 'bosses'. Television and the newspapers were was full of disputes. Naively in our non-industrial part of the world we thought this would not affect us, but then as the mining disputes grew ugly there were power cuts and the three-day working week was imposed to save fuel. Not even Hitler had done that to us and it was all the more morale sapping because it was self-inflicted. Two or three nights a week there would suddenly be no lights, no heating, and no television. Shivering by candlelight in one's own home it felt as if everything was breaking down. The world was going mad. Was anyone in charge? Clashes between the police and the miners escalated and there was a whiff of civil war in the air.

Although the coalfields were not strictly in our reporting area we soon became involved. George and I went to report on the picketing at our nearest pit, where thankfully there had been no violent clashes; we wondered what sort of reception we would receive. Leaving rural north Yorkshire we drove into a bleak industrial world. I felt even more depressed and then guilty. How could people live and work in this bleak environment of slag heaps with its rows of grim, mean, little terrace houses?

The pickets outside the pit gates were surprisingly friendly. George had put a big Press card in the car window hopefully declaring us as neutrals. The men were sitting around their oil drum fires waving placards and cheering whenever a car went by tooting its horn. As soon as they spotted our car there was animated chatter and a small group ran towards us. Thankfully there was excitement on the approaching faces not hostility.

'Has he resigned yet?' they shouted. Prime

Minster Heath had been making a statement in the Commons and we had been listening to it on the radio. It seemed only diplomatic to reply: 'Not yet.'

The excitement died down.

'Won't be long now, eh lads?' said one the men.

There were nods and growls of approval.

'We'll get rid of 'im and good riddance. Then we'll get things sorted.'

This was more than just a union dispute — they were intent on bringing down the government and they were as excited as schoolboys at the prospect. Didn't they realise what they were doing? What price chaos?

'Aren't you frightened of alienating a lot of people?' I said. 'I mean with the power cuts.'

'That's not our fault,' came a chorus of protests. 'Blame this bloody-minded Government for the power cuts not us! Give us our proper dues and we'll be back at work tomorrow.'

More nods and growls of approval all round.

'So the strike goes on?' I asked.

'Yeah! We'll have all the lights out in this country soon and then they'll have to go! Have to.'

And there were cheers and the waving of

fists. George took pictures of confident, determined mineworkers around their camp fires and I went home feeling even more apprehensive. Anarchy was in the air. When and how would it all end?

Prime Minister Heath called an election and we were thrown into the hurly burly of politics; that pushed my memories back to the first big political meeting I attended, as a teenager just after the war. One of the town's biggest cinemas was packed from the shilling seats at the front to the posh 'two and nines' upstairs. We all crowded in to hear J B Priestley, the famous Yorkshire author, speak. His was the warm reassuring voice we had all heard so often on the radio during the war and here he was in the flesh. 'Vote Labour', he said, so persuasively in his rich Yorkshire dialect that one felt it was not only right but our bounden Christian duty so to do. What had the Conservatives to offer he demanded? Just one tired old lion, Winston Churchill, but now it was a time of peace, a time for change! Change! It became the clarion call of the election.

Old JB held us all enrapured and there was a buzz of excitement as people streamed out of the cinema. There *was* going to be a change, you could feel it in the air, and when it came back in 1945 it was momentous

— Winston, the war hero, was defeated and Mr Attlee won.

Mr Heath however did not create that sort of excitement even though he posed a very valid question: who rules this country — the government or the unions?

44

George had cancer and that put things into perspective. His wife had died from the disease and outwardly he appeared to take the news about himself with extreme stoicism.

'Just keep playing a straight bat,' he said. 'Nothing more you can do — straight bat.'

He had a massive operation and was obviously in great pain when I visited him in hospital. There was sweat on his brow as we talked and I passed on everyone's concern for him.

'Thank them for all the cards and that,' he said and the sweat on his forehead grew heavier. 'Now clear off. You can't do any more here.'

This was typical of George, not one to waste time or words. Playing a straight bat ... I walked away from the hospital feeling sad, upset and annoyed. What right had I to feel dissatisfied with life?

When he came out of hospital, George rallied and the head office threw a party for him in a country pub. I took him there and it was a jolly affair full of jokes and happy reminiscences of jobs long gone by. Afterwards I drove him back to his starkly empty house. He made me a cup of tea and when it was drunk he said:

'Now get yourself back home and thanks for taking me.'

He wanted no talk or sympathy. He would play his straight bat all by himself.

Very soon he was taken into a private nursing home near the cathedral for terminal care, and during lunch-times I used to pop in to see him. He was sitting outside in the sun looking more gaunt and angular each day. I was far, far away on holiday when George died, but I had written a tribute to him before I left and it was used in the paper. We did not always agree but his death left a gap in all our lives.

★ ★ ★

The deepest and darkest of holes was being dug not too far away from the city but for once I was not showing any interest. The diggers were not looking for Vikings or Romans but were opening up a new coalfield at Selby. A deep vein of coal had been found underneath a rural part of the county and understandably the villagers sitting on top of it were nervous — they did not want to see slag heaps and pit winding-gear scarring their green fields; only a few miles south were grim examples of what coalfields could become. There was another fear carefully not put into words: how would country folk get on with all those flat-capped miners who would be pouring in to work in the new coalfield. And how would the miners get on with them?

In public consultations the National Coal Board had promised great things. There would be no spoil heaps and the traditional pit winding-gear would be in low towers; pit entrances and buildings would be shielded by banks of earth and trees. This was to be a coalfield hidden in a rural setting with the coal sliding out of the ground on a huge conveyor belt and being loaded onto trains running directly to the power stations. The countryside would not be raped as it had been elsewhere. The farmer on his tractor would not be held up by endless convoys of coal lorries blocking the lanes as he tried to get in the harvest. It all sounded very convincing and the nation did after all need coal.

This new mine story was full of superlatives and the industrial correspondents were having a field day. It was to be the largest deep mine coal project in the world with ten shafts linking 124 miles of underground roadways. All of this was on the edge of 'my patch' and I was quite happy to leave it there. It was therefore a surprise when I found that an invitation from the Coal Board had been passed on to me from head office. Would I like to go down the deepest hole in Europe? Knowing my interest in archaeological holes I think this was intended as a joke but in the spirit of adventure I accepted. I had never been down a coal mine, but of course it was not yet a coal mine — they were still boring the holes to make it into one. Dressed self-consciously in overalls and with miners' helmets on our heads, we all listened in subdued tones to the explanatory lecture. It was not reassuring. Half way down the shaft, we were told, the drillers had hit a water-bearing stratum of rock. I was alarmed. We were surely not going down a hole with water pouring in! No the problem had been solved. Special equipment had been installed which froze the water and the hole had continued going on down. There was still a ripple of unease among the overall-clad journalists. What if someone accidentally switched off the refrigerator?

In a dark shed we inspected the winding-gear on which our lives would soon depend and it looked reassuringly shiny and new. Steel cables went up above our heads and over a drum before going down into the shaft mercifully shielded from close inspection by a wire cage with a small door. The winding-gear sprang into life and for what seemed an eternity we watched the cables moving. How deep was deep? An unearthly glow came from the shaft as if the fires of hell were slowly rising up out of the depths to join us. But it was a huge bucket that appeared hung about with electric light bulbs. The door in the cage was opened and we climbed down a ladder into the bucket which was splattered with yellow mud and had water swilling about in the bottom. A dozen of us standing in the muddy water stared at each other hoping that fear was not showing in our faces. As we went down and down I imagined the growing distance between me and safety and my fear grew. How could people work down here for a living? The bucket stopped and swayed gently, banging against the sides. Our guide had something to tell us.

'This is the water-bearing section. As you can see it is frozen hard and quite safe.'

He picked up a telephone clamped to the side of our bucket.

'OK,' he said.

There was a jerk and we continued on our way down. I tried to come to terms with the possibility that I might never see the sky again. Lights appeared from below us, seeping up the gap between the shaft walls and our bucket. And then suddenly we were in a cave and light bulbs were blazing all around us and the air was suffocatingly hot. We were invited to climb out of our transport and down another ladder into the workings. All around us were men stripped to the waist operating drills and with water swilling everywhere. The noise and the heat added to the claustrophobia and the clammy, wet feeling of suffocation. We listened to our guide as he shouted details about how all the shafts would be linked up by miles of underground roads. No-one asked questions. No-one wanted to prolong our stay in the bowels of the earth any longer than necessary. We all edged back to our bucket.

'All OK? Seen enough?' shouted our guide. There were thumbs up all round. Slowly we ascended, every little bump on the side of the shaft causing momentary panic. We saw the sky again and I vowed that even if endowed with the necessary strength and courage I could never be a miner. How dare I moan about my job? How dare I feel dissatisfied?

The fresh air brought the journalists back to their loquacious selves. Photographers were begged to take pictures of everyone in their pit gear. Solidarity with the workers!

Pictures for the scrap book. I needed no photographs to remind me. I would never forget that 'cave' with its heat and noise and those sweating men and their drills. I revised my thoughts about miners. They deserved every penny they could get.

45

Great excitement — we were to have a royal visit. Prince Charles and his new wife were to pay a brief call to the National Railway Museum. The crowds turned out. We waited behind the VIPs in the entrance hall, watching through the glass doors as the people outside went wild. Prince Charles came in briskly with a palpably shy young lady trailing in his wake. All eyes were on her, beautiful and elegant, but looking so vulnerably young. Yet she smiled as she shook hands with the line of dignitaries before going inside to look at the steam trains.

For security reasons we were told we could not follow them but then the royal press officer appeared and said: 'Walk about. They've agreed to a walkabout in the street'.

The frustrated photographers were delighted and scuttled outside to find the best vantage points. When the royal couple reappeared they had split up. The Prince came first chatting to the museum director while the Princess was some way behind talking animatedly to a group of young officials. As the Prince was shaking hands with the director prior to leaving he realised that his wife was no longer with him. The keen young museum assistants were showing her some display cabinets at the other side of the room. The royal couple's eyes met and the prince's hand beckoned with just a touch of impatience. She said something to the young assistants, laughed, and half skipped and half ran across the room to join her husband. It was so gauche and little girl-like that everyone smiled. She had strayed and had been summoned and her response instantly endeared her to everyone.

Outside Prince Charles walked along the edge of the crowd exchanging banter and shaking hands but all eyes were looking over his shoulder at the shy young girl walking behind him.

★ ★ ★

Late night telephone calls boded ill. They always involved something unpleasant, a train crash or a multiple car pile-up so a call at 3.30am was particularly sinister. It was the cultured voice of the late duty sub-editor at Leeds.

'There appears to be some sort of a fire at the Minster,' he said very calmly. 'Perhaps you could check?'

I was suddenly very wide awake in my pyjamas.

'I will,' I said. 'But if it is something can you take copy.'

''Fraid not, old man. Morning paper's gone to bed and I'm just leaving myself. There's the evening paper to consider of course.'

There was indeed so in a great hurry I dressed and telephoned the fire brigade. Yes, the Minster was indeed on fire and it was serious. My heart gave an odd little jump. This was the 'big news' joke in the office. Anything happening? No, not much, just the Minster on fire.

I left Meriel on the telephone trying to raise the caretaker at an empty head office while I drove into the city ignoring all the speed limits.

York Minster was most certainly on fire. Fire engines filled the streets and hose-pipes criss-crossed the roadway like a forest of tree roots laid bare. Thousands of tons of water had been poured onto the blazing South Transept roof collapsing the burning timber and stopping the blaze spreading to the rest of the building. Knots of people were standing in the roadway staring upwards in disbelief. By some miracle the gable end of the transept with its stained glass window was intact. I joined a group of people gathered at the west end of the cathedral. One was the Archbishop of York, Dr John Habgood who was going to a conference in Geneva on an early morning flight and had been up and dressed when his telephone rang. With him was his lay chaplain who had not been quite so travel ready and was still wearing pyjamas under his coat. They were all looking in disbelief at the damage. They were joined by the fire chief coming out of the west door of the cathedral. The fire was out, he announced and he invited us inside to see for ourselves.

There was a deathly stillness inside the cathedral as if the building itself was stunned by what had happened. The floor of the great nave was swilling with water and smoke was drifting eerily along the high ceiling. The enormity of what had happened was only apparent on reaching the crossing at the end of the nave; the transept roof had gone and a pale mid-summer morning was breaking. The sun played over a smoking pile of black, charred beams splattered with molten lead, all that was left of the south transept roof. The scene was reminiscent of a wartime bombing raid.

Peter, the Minster glazier, was staring up at the 16th century Rose window that had survived and was murmuring: 'A moment of history, a moment of history,' which indeed it was.

All well and good, I thought, but I had

work to do. I interviewed the dean and heard how the clergy had rescued crucifixes and cloths from the high altar before being driven out of the cathedral by 'rain' — not the usual sort of rain but drips of molten lead from the burning roof. No-one had been hurt, but it had been a close-run thing — had the fire reached the 200ft high central tower, the whole cathedral might have been engulfed.

I scurried around getting eyewitness accounts and then reluctantly I left the smouldering cathedral and ran through the empty streets to the office; I rang Meriel. She had spoken to the caretaker at Leeds and he had got the evening paper's news editor out of bed. People were being called in for a special edition. As soon as a copy girl reached head office they would ring, I was told, meanwhile photographers were on their way.

So I typed out the biggest story of my life. There was no risk of making it over-dramatic because it was dramatic. The words poured out. I sat at my desk with the slips of copy piling up in front of me but the telephone did not ring. My biggest, best story ever was all written up but there was no-one to give it to! Suddenly the phone did ring: 'Evening Post copy,' said a bright, friendly voice that I knew well. At last!

'Oh it's you is it,' said the girl as I gave my

name. 'Old velvet tonsils himself.'

'What do you mean velvet tonsils?'

'We've got nick names for all you people, and that's yours, luv — velvet tonsils. Right; what have you got for us then.'

At the other end of the telephone my words were put on paper at lightning speed — how those girls could type! I spoke to the news desk — a special edition was being run as soon as the photographers returned and it would be rushed to the city. The aim was to beat the local newspaper onto the streets. The air of excitement was palpable.

I returned to the cathedral to gather more eyewitness accounts and I felt elated; I had got the story through and it was now up to them. The evening paper vans raced into the city at breakfast time and the paper was on sale with pictures; my name was writ large. We were first with the news! Hurrah! Scoop! Then I felt guilty. A disaster should not be a cause for celebration. Well, why not just a little celebration, after all the fire was not my fault. But whose fault was it? That was the question. Having satisfied the evening paper I realised that this was only just the beginning. The whole wide world was now alive to what had happened. This was no time to rest — the morning paper was awake and it was demanding copy. Find a new angle to the story they said. How had it happened? Who was to blame?

The popular theory was a lightning strike during a brief summer storm but soon something else was being talked about — someone to blame? A few days before the fire, the consecration had taken place in the cathedral of a new Bishop of Durham who in some quarters was regarded as a controversial figure because of his views on the Virgin Birth and the Resurrection. Was God showing his displeasure at the church's choice?

Church leaders quickly made it clear that while God moved in mysterious ways he was not in the habit of blasting cathedrals with thunderbolts just because he disapproved of a choice of bishop.

As the news of the fire spread the city seemed to go quiet, it felt subdued; the cathedral was its beating heart and the thought that it could so easily have been lost stunned everyone.

At the end of my longest day we had another shock, a pleasant one: Penny had an announcement to make: 'Mum, dad, I'm getting engaged.'

46

How the years go by with children: one moment they are toddlers holding your hand, then there are tears as they go off to university followed by pride when they graduate, and then anxiety, particularly for dads, when young men come courting. It was another of life's milestones but we were happy, Meriel particularly because now she had a wedding to organise.

I was distracted from wedding plans by the aftermath of the fire as important visitors poured in to survey the damage. One of the first was the Duchess of Kent whose white-rose wedding had been held in the cathedral. She was clearly appalled at the destruction and she broke all royal protocol by walking straight over to the little group of journalists reporting her visit.

'You must reassure people,' she told us. 'Tell them it will be rebuilt. And it will be even better than it was before.'

She was echoing the upsurge of determination and confidence already growing in the city. There were no doubts at all — it would be rebuilt. And that set me thinking. I remembered when the Central Tower was in danger of collapse and I had written thousands of words as the work progressed. Special supplements boosted circulation figures and they became yearly events. I became a word machine churning out supplements to be sold on street corners at 4p a copy. With the near collapse of the Central Tower and the work to save it some two million visitors had been attracted to the city by all the newspaper and television publicity. How many thousands more would be pulled in by the publicity created by this latest disaster? And how many more thousands of words would I have to write before the cathedral was rebuilt — 'better than it was before'.

★   ★   ★

An ornate, gold-embossed invitation card from the Admiralty in London drew my attention away from yet another follow-up story about the Minster. I was invited for drinks on board one of Her Majesty's ships on the occasion of its visit to the city. As we were more than 40 miles upriver this seemed unusual but an accompanying press release explained.

A Royal Navy vessel had never visited the city, even though a dozen ships had proudly

245

borne the name York. A visit was now possible because of the widening work carried out on some of the locks on the river. One of Her Majesty's smaller minesweepers would therefore squeeze her way up river to receive a civic welcome by the Lord Mayor. A press release explained that because of stringent licensing laws when the Royal Navy was in port, drinks could not be served but 'suitable refreshments will be available.'

York had been steeped in army traditions since the Romans, but had seen little of the Royal Navy and the Senior Service was clearly determined to put this right. The minesweeper was dazzling in fresh paint and the White Ensign fluttered defiantly. The shirts of the sailors manning the deck sparkled like those in a TV advert for washing powder. Even the rope alongside the gang-plank was a startling white.

I waved my Admiralty invitation and was welcomed aboard. A sailor directed me to a near-vertical metal ladder going below. A buzz of conversation hit me as I inserted myself carefully from above into the tiny ward-room which was already packed with people holding glasses and jammed so closely together that there was a grave risk of sipping from someone else's glass by mistake.

I glimpsed the Lord Mayor crushed into a

corner and with his gold chain of office almost entwined with the captain's medals. None of this detracted from the lively atmosphere and the animated conversation. A steward edged his way towards me.

'I'm afraid we can only offer you tea, sir. Would you like Typhoo or Mazawatti?'

It was a curious offer because no-one in the overcrowded ward room was drinking tea. The steward indicated a shelf with two huge glass flagons incongruously bearing tea labels. Beneath were pouring jugs and a selection of glasses. The contents of the flagons certainly did not look like tea and where was the tea-pot?

Puzzled I asked: 'Which would you recommend?'

'The Typhoo tastes very much like gin, sir, and they say the Mazawatti has a distinctive whisky flavour.'

'I'll try the Typhoo.'

'A very good choice sir.'

Considering the crush and the fact that we were almost having to take it in turns to breathe it was all acutely civilised. I fell into conversation with the nearest officer. We were pressed so embarrassingly close together that it would have been rude to do otherwise. I heard how the ship had reached the city with only inches to spare in the new locks. As he talked I sampled my half-full tumbler of cold 'tea' and it did taste suspiciously like gin — no wonder everyone was getting on so well.

I had looked up the history of the first ship to be called York and discovered it had not started off with that name at all. It had been a 52-gun frigate built in 1655 by the Roundheads and called Marston Moor after the battle they had convincingly won near the city. But when the Cavaliers took over again in 1660 the ship was renamed York. I was looking forward to telling the captain about this fascinating research but the compression of bodies and the limited rotation in the crowded ward-room never brought me within conversation range. Instead I sipped my 'tea' and learned all about mine-laying from the officer squeezed against me. Much later we all left in a very merry mood. The Royal Navy had done us and the city proud.

47

A nondescript brown envelope came through the post with some startling news that again took my mind off burning cathedrals. I had passed my A level examination in English Literature with a grade A. I was as pleased as an eighteen year old schoolboy. The evening classes, only two terms of them, had been great fun but we had spent so much time arguing about Antony, Cleopatra and Virginia Wolfe that we never got round to the poetry element of the exam at all.

'You'll just have to swan it,' said our young lady teacher. 'Poetry is only a small portion of the exam anyway.'

So we 'swanned it.' And now I had something to put in the blank spaces on a job application form; what job application form? Who was I kidding? At my age? Anyway one solitary A level would look pathetically lonely on an application form? Perhaps if I got another one — history maybe? Yes I would do that — I would enrol for another course in September. And now the Thatcher era was drawing to a close. It was 1990, and after seeing off the miners and the Argentinians in the Falklands, the mood was changing. People were marching again: 'Maggie, Maggie Maggie. Out! Out! Out!' Had any Prime Minister in this country ever left office without a dagger in their back?

Stacey and I were feeling low. Everything seemed to be in an unsettling state of flux. Sipping our coffee in Terry's tea-room we felt like a couple of old codgers trapped resentfully in a changing world. The only comfort was that we knew most of the other inhabitants in this graveyard of ambition and our advancing years and our local knowledge accorded us a degree of deference but should we be chasing fire engines at our age? Was this not a young person's game?

I had been trying to ease myself more into feature writing but I was still responsible for news gathering with all its daily pressures. And to make matters worse we were going to be computerised. No more cheery chats with the copy girls. We were two grumpy old men rebelling at change but still able to summon up a flicker of defiance.

'Hang onto this thought,' said Stacey. 'Until we give those damn computers some words to play they're just heaps of useless junk. They're nothing without us'.

He was right: we had to adapt, we had to embrace the new technology. Computers were just a tool, we told ourselves, a very clever typewriter with a filing cabinet attached. That's the spirit! A box of electronics was not going to tell us how to do our jobs!

A problem arose on the domestic front. I had by now acquired two A levels with my night school studies and had blithely embarked on a third course to give the long winter evenings a sense of purpose; I had also unthinkingly put my name down for the examination which was, after all in the coming year. Meriel spotted the problem.

'You do realise we are on holiday in Cornwall that week?'

'Ah,' I said.

'Yes ah,' said Meriel.

Months of reading and study were going to be wasted. Did it really matter? Yes it jolly well did matter but then again so did the family holiday. Something would have to be done but first those computers had to be confronted.

Every morning for a week I drove over to Leeds to face a bulky computer screen and the world weary explanations of a smug young reporter who had been given special tuition so he could teach the more senior members of staff. It was not as bad as I had expected, and I soon saw the advantages: articles could very easily be chopped and changed.

I remembered as a copy boy seeing elderly reporters surrounded by the crumpled rejects as they attempted to find an 'intro' to a complicated story. I recalled one reporter staring for ages at a blank sheet of paper in his typewriter before tearing that out too and throwing it away. Our typewriters were prized away from us — sturdy reliable old friends were dumped on the scrapheap. Underneath our desks writhed a mass of wires connected to mysterious black boxes which we were ordered not to touch on pain of electrocution. We nervously typed our first stories and saw them appear dancing across the computer screen; we pressed the right keys and the stories vanished but where to?

Disbelievingly we would ring the news desk: 'Have you got it?'

Profanities at the other end of the line.

'Of course we've got it. Stop wasting telephone calls.'

Sometimes the system crashed and a thousand-word article would vanish and experts had to be called to retrieve it from some electronic dark hole. But the monster infuriated me even more when it wagged its finger at me and told me that I had spelt something incorrectly. Who did it think it was?

48

The old Viking town of Jorvik was now emerging from the muddy ground in Coppergate with more and more houses, back garden privies, rubbish pits and work-shops being revealed. The stream of royal visitors from the old Viking lands continued and even Prince Charles came to take a look. There were official handouts and press briefings, TV camera crews and national reporters. 'My' holes in the ground were getting overcrowded and I childishly resented it, so I was glad when the time came to go on holiday. The sun was shining, lithe sun-tanned figures were surfing, children were exploring rock pools but I was sitting at a school desk staring at an overturned exam paper.

'You may look at your question papers now,' said the invigilator.

I was an honorary pupil at Penzance Grammar School thanks to my kind-hearted night-school teacher. She did not want my studies to be wasted and had written to the headmaster in Cornwall. To my surprise he agreed to accept me as a pupil as long as I produced my passport to prove my identity.

So here I was in a classroom with other pupils of Penzance Grammar who were far too nervous to be concerned about my presence.

I sat at the back cramped into my school desk and set about answering the questions. After three hours the invigilator told everyone to stop writing but a girl at a desk near me went on scribbling furiously. The invigilator repeated his instructions and the girl started to weep but went on writing. Everyone was embarrassed. The teacher waved us to the door and knelt down beside the girl talking softly. I felt guilty. What was I doing intruding into this world? I was on a silly ego trip but for these young people the whole course of their lives could have been set in those few hours at those desks. I went back to the holiday flat in St Ives feeling deflated and a little sad.

49

And now life was moving too fast. In top hat and tails I accompanied my daughter to the village church in a chauffeur-driven vintage car and I gave her away to the handsome young RAF officer who was waiting for her at the altar. Meriel did the catering for the reception in a marquee on the lawn and then the newlyweds drove off; my wife burst into tears and I tried hard not to do the same. Another milestone had just gone flashing by.

Back to work and with new young people coming into the office the generation gap was looming. We 'oldies' didn't watch the same programmes on television. We were not up with the latest slang phrases or the TV catchwords. I retreated into the world of archaeology and cathedral repairs.

The roof which had been destroyed by the fire went back on the south transept of the Minster. The great oak A frames were jointed and assembled in a vast tent behind the cathedral and hoisted into place by a giant crane. Inside the church we stared up at a new ceiling with glittering carved bosses decorating the joints of the ceiling ribs. I remembered when I had stood there, looking up and seeing nothing but sky; now it was all repaired and in a blink of an eye measured by the cathedral's own time-scale. Royalty visited to bestow its blessing on the restoration and we were crowded out yet again with television cameras and national reporters. Once again I felt stupidly protective. How many thousands of words had I written about this place over the years? Thousands and thousands of words . . .

But never mind that — what have you got for today's news list and tomorrow's and tomorrow's? It wasn't fun anymore. Disturbingly I found myself looking more and more backwards. How it had all changed. If that American marching band returned now and blasted its way once more through the narrow streets even the Dean would be out there applauding. I had seen the old city coming back to life and slowly realising that its age and history were assets that could be exploited, creating something magical that brought in the tourists who brought in the money for the new shops and restaurants that everyone could enjoy. My once sleepy overgrown village was now very much awake.

★   ★   ★

Mother died peacefully in her sleep; the cleaner lady had called in as usual and found her. Mother was nearly ninety but it was still a shock. We busied ourselves with the grim business of house clearing and house selling, distant relatives came for the funeral and there was one more journey to make to Wales where that little mountain was still watching and waiting.

When it was all over Meriel said to me:

'When?'

'When what?'

'When are you retiring or are you going to wait until this job kills you?

Certainly the death toll among my contemporaries had been rising. I had been attending too many subdued funerals of photographers and writers who had succumbed to heart attacks and other maladies; even a young editor had died in harness — our profession was not noted for longevity. I brooded morosely for retirement was now financially possible, so why was I staying on? Perhaps because it was one of those milestones that I was loath to admit that I had reached but did I want the daily pressure of working in a world that was getting younger and more competitive?

I put in my resignation. The paper invited me to a dinner where I was formally thanked for my services and given a gold watch. The local archaeological trust presented me with newly-struck silver 'Viking' coin in appreciation for my work publicising archaeology. That I liked — my quaint, old-fashioned obsession with archaeology had been appreciated after all.

And so I retired and the silence was deafening. Time stretched ahead of me without a single deadline in sight. I kept thinking morosely of all those paths not taken and wondering what if . . . ? Things kept happening in 'my' town and I reproached myself for not knowing about them first. Why for goodness sake? It was someone else's problem now. I knew what was happening: I was bored. Harry our university lecturer friend who was a great prober into people's souls sensed my ennui.

'Do something,' he said.

'Like what?'

'You've got three A levels — get yourself off to university.'

'That's ridiculous at my age.'

'No it's not. You've got the academic qualifications. I'll happily recommend you. Go for it.'

So I did. Instead of becoming an old age pensioner with a bus pass I became a full time student with a union card. But that of course is another story . . .

We do hope that you have enjoyed reading
this large print book.

Did you know that all of our titles
are available for purchase?

We publish a wide range of high quality
large print books including:
Romances, Mysteries, Classics
General Fiction
Non Fiction and Westerns

Special interest titles available in
large print are:
The Little Oxford Dictionary
Music Book
Song Book
Hymn Book
Service Book

Also available from us courtesy of
Oxford University Press:
Young Readers' Dictionary
(large print edition)
Young Readers' Thesaurus
(large print edition)

For further information or a free
brochure, please contact us at:
Ulverscroft Large Print Books Ltd.,
The Green, Bradgate Road, Anstey,
Leicester, LE7 7FU, England.
Tel: (00 44) 0116 236 4325
Fax: (00 44) 0116 234 0205

UNIVERSITY AT LAST!

John Scott

In his sixties John took early retirement, gave up journalism and decided it was time to fulfil a life-long ambition to get himself an education. He had already taken A-levels at night school, for fun, and found to his surprise that he had enough qualifications to become a full-time undergraduate at his home university — York. John describes the reactions of his wife, and the interactions of his fellow scholars, when instead of becoming an old age pensioner he became a student.

THE SECRET OF KIT CAVENAUGH

Anne Holland

Christian 'Kit' Cavenaugh, born in 1667 in Dublin, grew up on a Leixlip farm. A dragoon in the Marlborough Wars, Kit led an adventurous life, courting women, fighting duels and arguing a paternity suit before the truth became known: Kit was a woman. After her husband and father of her three children was press-ganged into the English army to fight in the European wars of the early eighteenth century, Kit disguised herself as a man and enlisted to find him. When she finally came face to face with him in 1704, she was enraged to find him in the arms of a Dutch woman. Kit's adventures did not end there . . .

TWO TURTLE DOVES

Alex Monroe

Growing up in 1970s Suffolk, in a crumbling giant of a house with wild, tangled gardens, Alex Monroe was left to wreak havoc by invention. Without visible parental influence, he made nature into his world. Creation became a compulsion, whether it was go-carts and guns, crossbows and booby-traps, boats, bikes or scooters. And then it was jewellery . . . From daredevil Raleigh bike antics and inter-schoolboy warfare, to the delicacies of dress-making and the most intricate metalsmithery, *Two Turtle Doves* traces the intimate journey of how an idea is transformed from a fleeting thought into an exquisite piece of jewellery.

THE LAST ENEMY

Richard Hillary

Richard Hillary was a dashing and handsome young man 'with all the luck' who enjoyed a privileged life in the Oxbridge culture of the 1930s. He trained as an RAF Spitfire pilot in World War II and was shot down in the Battle of Britain, unable to quickly escape from his burning aircraft and suffering extensive burns. In *The Last Enemy*, Hillary traces his extraordinary journey of recovery, which included undergoing pioneering plastic surgery to rebuild his face and hands. It was first published in 1942, just seven months before his untimely death in a second plane crash.

MUM'S LIST

St John Greene with Rachel Murphy

On her deathbed, Kate Greene's only concern was for her two little boys, Reef and Finn, and her loving husband, Singe. She knew she'd be leaving them behind very soon. Over her last few days, Kate created Mum's List to help the man she loved provide the best life for their boys after she was gone. It wasn't the first time Singe and Kate had faced the spectre of death. Four years earlier, doctors discovered a large lump in baby Reef's abdomen. Kate, pregnant with Finn, was so distressed that she gave birth dangerously early. Afterwards, Kate received the diagnosis that every woman dreads . . .